Business Intelligence and Data Warehousing Simplified

500 Questions, Answers, and Tips

Business Intelligence and Data Warehousing Simplified

500 Questions, Answers, and Tips

Arshad Khan

Mercury Learning and Information
Dulles, Virginia
Boston, Massachusetts

Publisher: David Pallai
Mercury Learning and Information
22841 Quicksilver Drive
Dulles, VA 20166
info@merclearning.com
www.merclearning.com
1-800-758-3756

This book is printed on acid-free paper.

Arshad Khan. Business Intelligence and Data Warehousing Simplified: *500 Questions, Answers, and Tips*.
ISBN: 978-1-936420-32-2

Library of Congress Control Number: 2011931634

111213321

CONTENTS

PREFACE

Business Intelligence and Data Warehousing Simplified: 500 Questions, Answers, and Tips is a primer for readers from diverse technical and nontechnical backgrounds who are interested in an introduction to business intelligence and data warehousing—an area that is currently in high demand despite a soft economy. This book, which is general and not tool based, will appeal to executives, managers, business analysts, developers, functional/subject matter experts (SMEs), and project implementation team members. It can also be used as a supplemental textbook for an introductory course in business intelligence or data warehousing.

Business Intelligence and Data Warehousing Simplified: 500 Questions, Answers, and Tips has been organized in a unique format: questions and answers are grouped by learning topics in a logical progression. Chapters include business intelligence application and future, data warehouse characteristics, star schema, architecture, metadata, data conversion and migration, ETL process, data marts, implementation approaches, multidimensionality, OLAP, common mistakes and risks, design, trends, and more. Wherever appropriate, tips and guidelines have been included.

I would like to take this opportunity to thank David Pallai, the publisher, for guiding this project to completion, despite many challenges, in a relatively brief period of time.

Arshad Khan

CHAPTER 1

INTRODUCTION

1 What is business intelligence?

Business intelligence (BI) is a decision support system, whose aim is to help make business decisions, strategic as well as operational/tactical. It uses an assortment of resources and techniques for gathering, transforming, storing, and analyzing data including the following:

- Processes
- Technologies
- Applications
- Quality
- Skills
- Practices
- Risks

The technologies utilized include data warehousing, online analytical processing (OLAP) or multidimensional analysis, data mining, analytical and statistical tools, querying and reporting tools, data visualization, dashboards, scorecards, among others. Together, various business intelligence technologies enable the following tasks, relevant to data and information, to be performed:

- Collection
- Integration
- Analysis

- Interpretation
- Presentation

Business intelligence is viewed differently by the two groups that use it—business and IT. Although IT usually views BI as a tool, business views it as information.

2 When was the term business intelligence introduced?

The term "business intelligence" was first coined in 1958 by IBM® researcher, Hans Peter Luhn, in the IBM Journal article titled "A Business Intelligence System" (*https://www-927.ibm.com/ibm/cas/toronto/projects/projects*). According to his definition, business intelligence refers to "the ability to apprehend the interrelationships of presented facts in such a way as to guide *action* toward a *desired goal*." Analyzing this definition emphasizes two key points:

- Desired goal –indicates a direct link to performance management
- Action –refers to decision making for achieving the desired goal

3 How can business intelligence be defined?

There is no single universally used definition of business intelligence. In 1989, Howard Dresner defined "business intelligence" as encompassing "concepts and methods to improve business decision making by using fact-based support systems" (*http://en.wikipedia.org/wiki/Business_intelligence*).

In 1996, Gartner® elaborated with the following description:

> By 2000, Information Democracy will emerge in forward-thinking enterprises, with Business Intelligence information and applications available broadly to employees, consultants, customers, suppliers, and the public. The key to thriving in a competitive marketplace is staying ahead of the competition. Making sound business decisions based on accurate and current information takes more than intuition. Data analyses, reporting,

> and query tools can help business users wade through a sea of data to synthesize valuable information from it—today these tools collectively fall into a category called "Business Intelligence" (*http://searchdatamanagement.techtarget.com/definition/business-intelligence*).

The following definition can be found at the SearchData Management.com Web site:

> Business intelligence (BI) is a broad category of applications and technologies for gathering, storing, analyzing, and providing access to data to help enterprise users make better business decisions. BI applications include the activities of decision support systems, query and reporting, online analytical processing (OLAP), statistical analysis, forecasting, and data mining (*http://searchdatamanagement.techtarget.com/definition/business-intelligence*).

4 What is the relationship between business intelligence and data warehousing?

In the current environment, business intelligence and data warehousing are used synonymously. Most data warehouse vendors now promote their products as business intelligence software, rather than data warehouse software. In practical terms, a data warehouse is the infrastructure component of a popular and widely used system that is implemented to achieve business intelligence.

According to *The Forrester Wave™: Enterprise Business Intelligence Platforms, Q4 2010*, by Boris Evelson et al. (Forrester® Research Inc., October 20, 2010), business intelligence is often defined in one of two ways:

> Typically, we use the following broad definition: Business intelligence is a set of methodologies, processes, architectures, and technologies that transform raw data into meaningful and useful information used to enable more effective strategic, tactical, and operational insights and decision-making. When using this definition, BI also has to include technologies such as data

> integration, data quality, data warehousing, master data management, text, and content analytics, and many others that the market sometimes lumps into the information management segment. Therefore, we also refer to data preparation and data usage as two separate, but closely linked, segments of the BI architectural stack. We define the narrower BI market as: A set of methodologies, processes, architectures, and technologies that leverage the output of information management processes for analysis, reporting, performance management, and information delivery.

As this definition indicates, data warehousing is a technology that is included in business intelligence. However, it needs to be noted that although data warehouses provide data to business intelligence applications, all BI applications are not dependent on data warehouses to provide them with the data that they need.

5 What is operational BI?

Business intelligence has historically been focused on strategic decision making and analytics. Operational business intelligence, or operational BI, aims to provide information and insights that are operation-focused, with a time frame that can extend from near real-time to a few years. Its objective is to enable decision making that focuses on day-to-day operations rather than strategic decisions which, previously, was the primary focus of business intelligence. Operational business intelligence benefits an extensive range of users who, sometimes within minutes or a few hours, can use it to run, manage, or optimize time-sensitive business operations.

6 Which tools are used for business intelligence?

A number of tools are available for business intelligence applications. These can fit into five broad categories: reporting, analytics, dashboards, alerts, and data integration. The most widely used are the reporting tools, which include commercial reporting tools as well as custom developed tools. They provide reasonable flexibility to most users so that they can create, modify, and schedule their reports within IT or business-specified constraints.

Dashboards are popular mechanisms for displaying reports, especially summarized ones, and performance metrics. Advanced users, especially those who need multidimensional analysis, prefer OLAP tools. Sophisticated users—those who need very unique and in-depth analysis—prefer to use data mining and statistical tools. The most popular tool is Excel®, which is inexpensive and can provide low-level analysis. Most reporting tools provide a feature to export results into Excel, where additional analyses can be performed.

7 What are the different styles of business intelligence?

Business intelligence can also be categorized into various styles. The most commonly referenced is the categorization provided by MicroStrategy®, which includes the following:

- Scorecards and dashboards
    - Aimed at providing executives and managers at-a-glance information in a visually appealing, summarized format
- Enterprise reporting
    - Aimed at all users, with more detailed operational data and focused information provided
- OLAP analysis
    - Provides analytical capabilities, such as slicing and dicing, drilling, pivoting, etc., for managers and business users
- Advanced predictive analysis
    - Enables business analysts and power users to perform predictive and statistical analyses against summarized, as well as detailed, data
- Alerts and proactive notification
    - Provides reports to all types of users and distribution lists based on exceptions, deviations, preset schedules, as well as ad hoc distribution requirements

Another categorization is based on the following:

- Enterprise
  - Complex and expensive; dominated by large companies like SAP® BusinessObjects™
- Windows®
  - Characterized by locked platform and lack of competition; dominated by Microsoft®
- Web and XML
  - Characterized by open standards, agility, and smaller companies like LogiXML™
- Open-Source
  - Free and characterized by expensive maintenance, lack of support, and smaller companies like Jaspersoft®
- SaaS
  - Characterized by simplicity, ease of use, lack of flexibility, higher risk, and smaller companies like PivotLink

8 How large is the business intelligence market?

According to the Gartner report *Market Share: Business Intelligence, Analytics and Performance Management Software, Worldwide, 2009*, the worldwide business intelligence analytics and performance management revenue estimate for 2009 was $9.3 billion. Of this amount, 64.25% or approximately $6 billion was estimated for the business intelligence platform segment, which represented a growth of 4.8% over the previous year. In 2010, worldwide spending on business intelligence analytics and performance management applications, according to Gartner, had increased to $10.5 billion—a 13% increase (*www.cio.com*, May 15, 2011).

9 Who are the most significant business intelligence vendors?

Gartner has identified visionaries, leaders, challengers, and niche business intelligence vendors in its Magic Quadrant, which is shown in Figure 1 (*Gartner RAS Research Note G00210036*).

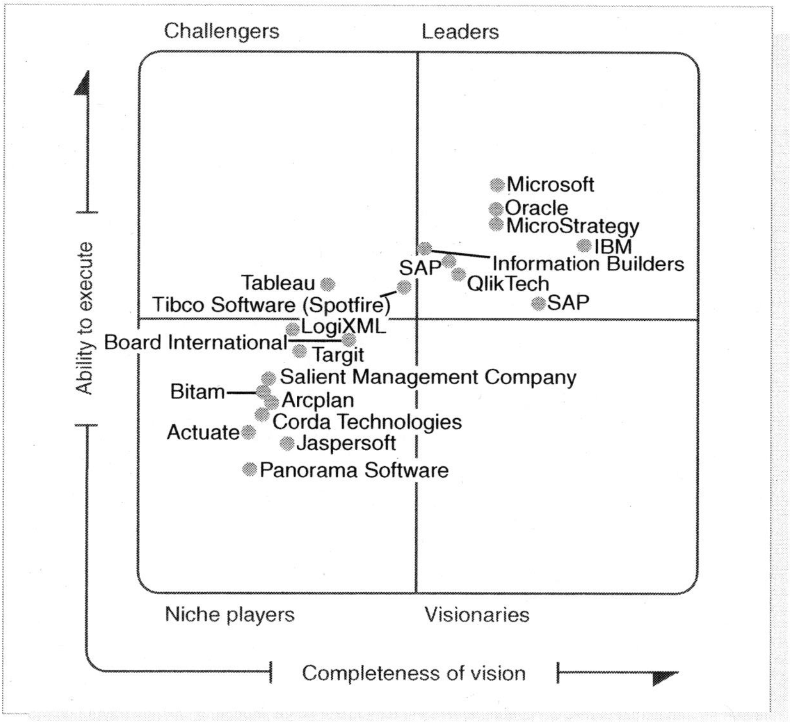

FIGURE 1 Magic Quadrant for business intelligence platforms.

The Gartner report also states that the largest business intelligence vendors are SAP, Oracle®, SAS®, IBM®, and Microsoft. Their market shares are displayed in Table 1.

TABLE 1 Business Intelligence, Analytics, and Performance Management Revenue

Company	**2009 Revenue (in million dollars)**
SAP	2,084.1
Oracle	1,351.1
SAS Institute	1,324.6
IBM	1,135.6
Microsoft	739.1
MicroStrategy	295.0
Others	2,392.4
Total	9,321.9

Table data is from 2009 and might not represent Gartner's current view of the marketplace.

CHAPTER 2

BUSINESS INTELLIGENCE APPLICATION AND FUTURE

10 Where can business intelligence be applied?

Business intelligence applications can be categorized in many ways, as the following listing of commonly implemented business intelligence applications demonstrates:

- Operations reporting
  - Provides information about routine business operations and benchmarking
- Strategic reporting
  - Focuses on the strategic objectives of the enterprise, using tools such as OLAP and data visualization
- Multidimensional analysis
  - Provides insight, through slicing and dicing, into data at various granularity levels
- Analytics
  - Includes an array of techniques for optimizing decision making, such as predictive analysis, statistical analysis, and so forth
- Forecasting
  - Provides a forecast or estimate of what to expect in the future, based on the extrapolation of historical data

- Correlation
  - Determines how various variables can be related using techniques such as data mining
- Dashboards
  - Used for presenting reports and key performance indicators (KPIs) at a glance, with the ability to drill down to the underlying data
- Collaboration:
  - Enables various functional areas, inside and outside the company, to work together

The spectrum of applications and functions covered by business intelligence includes managed reporting, ad hoc reporting, interactive data visualizations, predictive analysis, data integration, business performance management, text mining, information widgets, customer profiling, market segmentation, revenue, sales, profitability, among others.

11 What are the benefits of business intelligence?

There are many benefits of business intelligence that are also applicable to data warehousing. The following are some of the benefits that can be associated with both:

- Support strategic and operational decision making
- Provide timely information
- Enable data and process integration, internally and externally
- Enable easy and powerful data analysis, across current and historical periods
- Streamline business processes and provide decision support for them
- Enable insight into business trends and opportunities
- Provide competitive advantage, through improved knowledge about the business and competition

- Generate new revenue
- Reduce costs (improved processes)
- Improve the bottom line (profits)
- Help to increase and/or retain customers
- Enable users, who are freed from IT dependence, to analyze data from different angles, using powerful front-end access tools
- Support ad hoc as well as managed reporting
- Provide more accurate and complete information, enabling "one version of the truth"

12 Who are business intelligence beneficiaries?

Business intelligence applications are now being used, by a very wide variety of users, at every level in the corporate hierarchy. From business reporting for a select few, business intelligence has now become a tool for the masses. Its users include the following groups:

- Strategic and operational users
- Traditional users of decision support systems
- Top-, middle-, and junior-level managers
- Line managers
- Front-tier workers
- Business analysts
- Information workers
- Novice and casual users
- Power/super users
- IT and developers
- Customers
- Partners
- Suppliers

13 How varied are the needs of business intelligence users?

The needs of users vary considerably because their information requirements and abilities vary considerably. For example, the different needs can include the following abilities:

- Execute easy-to-use queries and reports, with few parameters, if the user is not technology savvy
- Generate periodic reports for analyzing variances
- Crunch numbers, slice and dice, and manipulate data and report results
- Access and navigate dashboards and execute embedded reports

The following are examples of how varied the needs can be for different classes of users:

- Savvy analyst
  - Performs sophisticated analyses, which might include statistical analysis, data mining, etc.
- Information subscriber
  - Receives reports executed by other users or the system
- Executive
  - Receives summarized strategic results
- Report writer
  - Builds complex reports
- Manager
  - Needs daily reports and the ability to drill down

14 Should business intelligence be designed for IT or non-IT users?

There are two sides of business intelligence: technology and business. When a business intelligence project is initiated by IT, the business tends to receive less attention than it should. Often decisions are made that are more beneficial to IT than to the business, which is the ultimate consumer of the finished product. A business intelligence system should always be designed with the paramount objective of meeting the needs of the business users if it is to provide maximum benefit to the organization.

15 What is Business Intelligence 2.0 (BI 2.0)?

Business intelligence has evolved, in the past few years, to incorporate the utilization of new software and tools that extend its capabilities, rather than replace them. The new features and capabilities of BI 2.0, which has been defined in a number of ways, include the following:

- Real-time insight through dynamic querying of real-time data
- Collaboration
- Convergence
- Agile analysis
- Reducing the time gap between analysis and action
- Search
- Visualization
- Universal availability
- Enterprise data integration, through master data management (MDM) and other technologies
- Hardware and software integration, via appliances and other tools
- Web-based approach and delivery
- Service-oriented architecture (SOA)
- Software-as-a-service
- Embedded BI
- Advanced analytics
- Integration with business processes and tools

- Performance management and integrated planning
- Encompasses vendors, customers, and others beyond the corporate boundaries
- Mission critical applications
- Open source
- Unstructured data

16 What is the future of business intelligence?

Companies continue to have decision support and performance issues because of the lack of information and tools. According to the 2010 CIO survey by Gartner Executive Programs (EXP), business intelligence ranked fifth in the list of the top ten business and technology priorities in 2010 (*http://www.gartner.com/it/page.jsp?id=1283413*). In a global CIO survey of 209 IT executives, regarding the primary ways their companies planned to innovate in 2011, 24% selected "Get better business intelligence to more employees, faster" (*Informationweek*, March 14, 2011, p. 30). These, along with the continued focus on cutting costs and improving productivity, are good indicators that business intelligence will continue to remain an important technology for many more years.

The growth in business intelligence will be apparent in some of the current trends. For example, it is expected that there will be an increase in the use of software-as-a-service, as companies try to obtain business intelligence capabilities without being encumbered with the implementation and support of a BI infrastructure. Other trends in the business intelligence space include advanced analytics, cloud computing, unstructured data analysis, visualization, and so forth, which are described in more detail in "Trends," the last chapter of this book.

CHAPTER 3

DATA WAREHOUSING EVOLUTION AND FUNDAMENTALS

17 How have information-processing requirements evolved?

The task of obtaining any meaningful data or information from the early computer systems used to be very tedious. Consequently, a number of methods, techniques, and tools have been developed to solve that problem. These include decentralized processing, extract processing, executive information systems (EIS), query tools, relational databases, and so forth. The need for timely and accurate decisions also has led to the development of decision-support systems, ranging from simple to very sophisticated systems. The data warehouse is the latest tool in this evolution.

18 What were the consequences of multiple applications and platforms?

Traditional business applications were designed and developed with the objective of helping specific departments or functions such as marketing, human resources, finance, inventory management, loan processing, among others. Because such applications were typically developed independently and without coordination, over a period of time, they often collected redundant data. Also, the data residing in these applications, which were often developed on different platforms, were incompatible and inconsistent. Consequently, there was poor data management, enterprise view of data was lacking, and, frequently, a query would return varied results depending on the application that was accessed and analyzed.

What made the situation even worse after 1981, when the personal computer (PC) was developed, was the explosion in the number of systems as well as the quantity and types of data being collected. The loss of a central data repository coincided with the widespread demand for timely and increased information.

19 What were the limitations of transaction-processing systems?

Online transaction processing (OLTP) systems were developed to capture and store business operations data. Because robustness was their top priority, rather than reporting or user accessibility, they suffered from some serious limitations. Their most obvious shortcomings were the inability to address the business users' need to access stored transaction data and management decision-support requirements in a timely fashion. OLTP systems also did not address history and summarization requirements or support integration needs (the ability to analyze data across different systems and/or platforms).

20 When was data warehousing conceptualized?

The failure of OLTP systems to provide decision-support capabilities ultimately led to the data warehousing concept in the late 1980s. Its objective, in contrast to OLTP systems, was to extract information instead of capturing and storing data, and hence, it became a strategic tool for decision makers. At this time, data warehousing strives to become the foundation of corporate-wide business reporting and analytics by becoming the enterprise information hub, supporting both tactical and strategic decision making.

21 Does the arrival of data warehousing herald the end of decentralization?

In a way, the data warehouse concept has involved traversing a full circle. After the PC was invented, islands of data had sprouted in a move of independence, away from the centralized mainframe concept.

The data warehouse, by collecting data stored in disparate systems, is a return to the centralized concept. A key difference exists, however; a data warehouse enables enterprise as well as local decision-support needs to be met, while permitting independent data islands to continue flourishing. It provides a central validated data repository, which can provide "one version of the truth," while supporting the satellite systems that it feeds.

22 What is a data warehouse?

The term "business data warehouse" was coined in the late 1980s by IBM researchers Barry Devlin and Paul Murphy (*http://en.wikipedia.org/wiki/Data_warehouse*). According to Bill Inmon, better known as the father of data warehousing, "a data warehouse is a subject oriented, integrated, non-volatile, and time-variant collection of data in support of management's decisions" (*Building the Data Warehouse*, W.H. Inmon, John Wiley & Sons, Inc., p. 29).

In practical terms, a data warehouse is a large analytical database, which is populated from a variety of source systems that typically run the business. It acts as the corporate-centralized repository where consistent, detailed, summarized, current, as well as historical data is stored. It contains transaction as well as non-transaction data and is designed for querying, reporting, and analysis. The data in a data warehouse can be accessed, flexibly and interactively, using a variety of front-end, easy-to-use, data-access and data-mining tools.

23 What are the benefits of a data warehouse?

Many benefits that are associated with business intelligence, identified previously, are also associated with data warehouses. Additional benefits of data warehousing include the following:

- Despite leveraging multiple data sources, a data warehouse provides a common data model that enables easier reporting and analysis across the enterprise.
- Because they contain clean, validated data, reports and analyses that run against data warehouses are trusted.
- Because data is stored for very long periods, it enables trending and historical comparisons over longer periods.

- Data can be retrieved more efficiently than it can by an operational system, because a data warehouse is designed for retrieving data—not for writing data to the database.
- Data warehousing can work, and be integrated, with other applications such as enterprise resource planning (ERP) and customer relationship management (CRM).

24 What are the shortcomings of data warehousing?

Data warehouses also have some disadvantages, such as the following:

- Most data warehouses do not have current data because of the extraction, transformation, and loading (ETL) process, which is typically based on a daily loading schedule except in the case of real-time systems. Hence, data can be out of sync between the data warehouse and the operational OLTP system, which can cause reports executed in the different systems to return different results. In most cases, this is not an issue as long as the users are trained and made aware of the loading schedule.
- Though they handle structured data quite well, the use of unstructured data in data warehouses is limited or nonexistent.
- Enterprise data warehouse (EDW) systems are very expensive to implement and maintain.
- Business changes can be rapid, which can make it a challenge to keep the data warehouse system up to date because implementing quick changes is not easy, for technical as well as business reasons.

CHAPTER 4

DATA WAREHOUSE TYPES AND DESIGN OBJECTIVES

25 What are the different types of data warehouses?

There are three types of data warehouses:

- Enterprise data warehouse (EDW)
- Data mart
- Operational data store (ODS)

26 What is an enterprise data warehouse?

An enterprise data warehouse (EDW) contains data extracted from an organization's different systems, such as ERP and CRM, which run its business. A typical company can have anywhere from 5 to 20 systems feeding its EDW. Such an EDW contains detailed transaction data as well as summarized data. The data stored in such a data warehouse, which is organized according to subjects such as sales or inventory, can range from a couple of years to more than 20 years. This period is determined by the organization's business requirements. The volume of data stored in an EDW can range in the hundreds of gigabytes or terabytes. Many data warehouses now contain data volumes that are in the petabyte range.

27 What is a data mart?

A data mart is a small data warehouse that aims to meet the needs of departments and smaller groups, rather than the enterprise. It contains only a subset of the enterprise data. A data mart is defined by the functional scope of its users—not by the size of the data mart.

The design principles and objectives of a data mart and a data warehouse are the same. Although both are decision-support tools and have the same basic characteristics, such as being subject-oriented and integrated, a data mart is far smaller in size and scope. Typically, it is limited to one or two subjects (such as sales and finance). An enterprise can have many data marts. The source system that provides data to a data mart can be a data warehouse, another data mart, or an OLTP system.

A data mart, like a data warehouse, can include both detailed and summarized data. It can be fed from multiple systems. It uses far fewer data sources compared with a data warehouse, however, whose data volume is significantly larger. A typical data mart will contain less than 100 gigabytes of data. A data mart requires simpler hardware and a supporting technical infrastructure. Hence, it can be implemented by less experienced staff (who have limited technical skills) within months—and at a far lower cost, compared with a data warehouse.

28 What is an operational data store?

An operational data store (ODS) is a subject-oriented database that contains structured data extracted directly from operational transaction system data sources. Usually, it will contain very little summarized and historical data. An ODS is stored independently of the production system database. It contains current—or near current—data, and its objective is to meet the ad hoc query, tactical day-to-day needs of operational users. An ODS is also used as a staging area before data is imported into a data warehouse. In contrast to a data warehouse, which contains static data, an ODS can be frequently updated from operational systems—even in real-time.

29 What differentiates OLTP and data warehouse applications?

Operational (OLTP) systems are primarily used to run a company's business. They are transaction based, and they support business applications such as procurement, inventory, sales, order management, accounting, human resources, and so forth. Such systems require fast access, which is usually predefined, to the database where the data is stored. However, data warehouses focus on analytics, including multidimensional data analysis, and the ability to run ad hoc reports. Such systems are flexible and provide the ability to drill down, slice and dice, etc. Whereas the operational systems and applications are performance driven, data warehouses require flexibility rather than speed.

The characteristics of OLTP data and data warehouse data are also quite different. For example, the characteristics that define data warehouse data include high redundancy, flexible structure, and large data volumes; also, they are analysis and management oriented, and they permit ad hoc access. This is in contrast to OLTP data, which is defined by detailed data that is transaction driven, is updated continuously, has smaller data volumes, has no redundancy, and is readily available and highly reliable.

30 What is the design objective in OLTP systems?

An OLTP relational database is a collection of two-dimensional tables, which are organized into rows and columns. In such a database, the design objective is to optimize table structures by eliminating all instances of data redundancy. This is achieved by making database tables as small as possible and, when required, merging selected tables through joins. Therefore, such a system contains a very large number of small tables in which there is minimum data redundancy.

31 What is the design objective in data warehouse systems?

In a data warehouse, the design objective is the opposite of an OLTP system. The aim is to make more of the data available in fewer tables, with a great deal of redundancy that makes the database tables very large, which minimizes the need for table joins when a query is executed. The objective is to enable a query to find most of its required data in a single table, which will reduce the volume of data that will need to be pulled from other tables. The technique of merging small tables into larger tables with data redundancy, called **denormalization**, causes fewer input/output operations, which improves query performance. Denormalization, although suitable for a data warehouse, is not appropriate for a transaction database that emphasizes performance over query processing.

32 In which areas are data warehouse applications implemented?

Data warehousing has gone mainstream and it is being applied across all types of industries and functions by small as well as large companies. Its implementation mirrors the areas of application of business intelligence, which were listed previously, including operational and strategic reporting, multidimensional analysis, forecasting, trend analysis, marketing, sales, financial operations, customer profiling, fraud analysis, and logistics.

CHAPTER 5

GROWTH CONTRIBUTORS

33 What has contributed to the growth of data warehousing?

Data warehousing, which began growing explosively in the mid-1990s, is still characterized by relatively high growth. It is now considered to be a mainstream strategic tool that a competitive organization cannot afford to ignore. There are many reasons for the growth and widespread implementation of data warehousing; these are explained in the following sections.

34 Shift in focus from data to information

In the past, companies focused on capturing and storing business data, rather than analyzing it. Therefore, management lived with IT-provided standard canned reports, which often were not provided in a timely manner. In the past three decades, however, as corporate needs changed and quick decision-making became required, management shifted its focus from collecting and storing data to extracting information. When it realized that the required information could not be extracted quickly or easily from the OLTP systems, management began to explore various potential solutions, including data warehousing.

35 Emergence of key business drivers

The emergence of a number of key business drivers, as well as many enabling technologies, has fueled the growth of data warehousing. These key business drivers, which developed from the need to compete more effectively in a very competitive environment, included the following:

- Growing demand for information at every level in the corporate hierarchy
- Need for increasing efficiency and productivity
- Need to control costs
- Need to increase revenues
- Shift from capture and storing data to analyzing data
- Need to leverage corporate data and its hidden value
- Data proliferation and need for analysis
- Strategy that enabled self-service for information access

36 Increase in the competitive environment

In the past couple of decades, American corporations have faced tremendous pressure from low-cost producers to become more competitive and to improve their productivity. As part of their effort to achieve a competitive edge—to become "lean and mean"—companies began to look more closely at the data that they had collected over the years. Their need to analyze the huge volumes of collected data, which was scattered in disparate systems, led to the explosive growth in data warehousing.

37 Trend toward globalization

The globalization of the world economy in the past two decades has forced American companies to compete with foreign companies, which had been providing relatively low-cost goods and services. Many American manufacturers could not compete in the new environment and, consequently, they had to cease operations or move them to Third World countries. The only way that American companies could compete in the new environment was by becoming more efficient and by improving their productivity. To achieve these objectives, they made a serious attempt to use various technologies, including data warehousing.

38 Push for innovation and efficiency

During the economic downturns that occurred in the 1980s and 1990s, American companies downsized considerably and made serious efforts to reengineer their businesses. Continuous and never ending changes in the business environment has forced management to become innovative and to make the best use of their resources—humans as well as data—which has contributed to data warehousing growth. The importance that companies have given to their business intelligence initiatives can be gauged from the decision that a billion-dollar company took in early 2009, at the height of the financial crisis. While projects were being chopped right and left, the company doubled its data-warehouse-project budget because it wanted to control costs and improve revenues through better data analysis, which enabled it to improve its profitability and the bottom line.

39 Exponential increase in desktop power

The power of PCs nowadays is greater than the mainframes of a few years ago. The PC has evolved from a personal productivity tool, which was initially used for word processing and simple spreadsheet calculations, to one that supports sophisticated business applications and heavy-duty multidimensional analysis. This evolution has led to it being used as the primary tool for accessing data warehouses. Without the PC, the widespread use of data warehouses by end-users, who now are quite technology savvy, would not have been possible.

40 Technology developments: Software and hardware

A number of technology developments have contributed to data warehousing growth:

- Software characterized by many desirable features including
    - Reliability
    - Affordable cost
    - Easy and fast installation
    - Support for virtual memory

    - Multitasking
    - Symmetrical multiprocessing (SMP)
- Hardware enhancements including
    - Symmetric multiprocessors
    - Massively parallel processors (MPP)
- Improvements in relational database management system (RDBMS) features and technology
- Middleware development
- Widespread growth in networks
- Graphical user interface (GUI) tools

41 Widespread availability of integrated application software

The widespread use of ERP software from SAP, Oracle, and others led to the collection of huge volumes of transaction data. However, even though ERP software has been very efficient in collecting data, it has fallen short of satisfying the varied reporting needs of its users. Therefore, to meet their need for flexible reporting, many companies have been forced to build a data warehouse following an ERP implementation.

42 Proliferation of data

The amount of data being collected by corporations has grown by leaps and bounds in the past three decades. Some of the most significant contributors of data proliferation have been e-Commerce, the Internet, and clickstream data. Therefore, there has been a widespread push to analyze the data collected from these systems. The tool of choice for this purpose has been the data warehouse.

43 Growth of Internet and Intranets

The explosive growth of the Internet as well as Intranets, which are company networks based on Internet standards, has also fueled data-warehousing growth. The ability to access a data warehouse through a Web browser or a smartphone, from any location, has eliminated the need to install or learn complex data-access software and tools. Consequently, it has significantly increased the number of users, with varied requirements, who also create data as they browse the Internet or the Intranet.

44 Rapid decline of hardware prices

An important factor in widespread data warehouse deployment and use has been the sharp decline in the price of computer hardware, especially storage, even as computer processing power and capacity has increased tremendously. Prices of processors, disk drives, memory, and peripherals have dropped dramatically in the past few years, and, consequently, data-warehouse hardware has become more affordable.

45 End-users becoming more technology savvy

The introduction of the PC has led to business users becoming more comfortable with computer technology. Their level of knowledge and sophistication has enabled them, across the corporate world, to become fairly independent of programmers and systems analysts for their analytical and reporting needs. Such users are able to use sophisticated software tools with minimal training. Additionally, there has also developed a large pool of technology-savvy business analysts who are as comfortable with technology as they are with business. Such users have been instrumental in the widespread and efficient utilization of data warehouses.

CHAPTER 6

DATA WAREHOUSE CHARACTERISTICS

46 What are the basic characteristics of a data warehouse?

A date warehouse, as described by Bill Inmon, is characterized by four unique data characteristics:

- Subject-oriented
- Integrated
- Time-variant
- Nonvolatile

47 What is the subject-oriented characteristic?

The data in a data warehouse is organized according to subjects such as customer, vendor, bookings, orders, and products. This contrasts with classical applications that are organized by business functions such as loans, finance, inventory, and the like. In a data warehouse, the major subject areas are physically implemented as a series of related database tables. A data warehouse can contain a few, scores, or even hundreds of subject areas, depending on how widely it has been implemented within the enterprise. Examples of subject areas include revenue, service, bookings, billings, backlog, invoicing, sales, margins, and executive, among others.

48 What is the integrated characteristic?

The data in a data warehouse is always integrated—without any exception. The source data from multiple systems is consolidated in a data warehouse after undergoing various operations such as extraction, transformation, and loading. The data imported from the source systems reflects integration through consistent naming conventions, data attributes, data definitions, measurements, and so forth. A data warehouse can contain data integrated from a few or even hundreds of systems, depending on how widely it has been implemented within the enterprise.

49 What is the time-variant characteristic?

Data warehouse data is accurate as of a moment in time, whereas transaction data is accurate as of the moment of access. The data in a data warehouse consists of a lengthy series of snapshots, taken at various points in time, which can cover a very lengthy period that can stretch from 5 to 20 years. In contrast, typical transaction databases contain data for a period of only 6 to 24 months. The time-variant characteristic enables data to be trended over various periods. It also enables data to be compared over different periods, such as revenue growth year-over-year or change in the average selling prices month-over-month.

50 What is the nonvolatile characteristic?

The data stored in a data warehouse remain static, in other words, read-only. Any new data, which is typically introduced periodically, is appended. Data warehouse data is subjected to regular access and analysis. However, activities such as insertions and deletions, which occur routinely with operational systems, do not occur in a data warehouse, which is initially populated through a massive data load from the source systems, followed by periodic appends. After data has been introduced into a data warehouse, users can only analyze it—not change it. The only time data is changed in a data warehouse is when a data error is discovered and needs rectification.

51 What are the characteristics of an OLTP database?

An OLTP database contains detailed transaction data, which is collected from the organization's business operations. Though such a database might contain some derived data, which is calculated from the basic data elements, it primarily comprises basic data elements at the lowest granular level. For example, the primary element can be the sales price, whereas the derived data can be the item's average sales price over a period of time. An OLTP transaction database runs the business and is optimized for update functions—not for querying and analysis. Its data is structured and organized so that it favors performance and speed for capturing business transactions (through normalization and an entity-relationship model), reliability, data integrity, and security. The database contains small tables because it has to capture data efficiently, as performance is an overriding factor. An OLTP database collects a large volume of raw transaction data that cannot be analyzed easily. Such a database does not address decision support requirements of history, summarization, integration, and metadata.

OLTP systems are not used as repositories of historical data, which is required for analyzing trends. Typically, such systems have inconsistent, dynamic (rapidly changing), as well as duplicate and/or missing entries. Also, the data in transaction databases is not in a form that is meaningful to end-users.

52 What are the characteristics of a data warehouse database?

A data warehouse database contains transaction data that has been restructured, and denormalized, for querying and analysis. It contains detailed granular data, and derived data, as well as aggregated data. The availability of detailed data permits drill-down to be performed, if there is a need to dig deeper after the summarized data has been reviewed. For example, a manager can initially analyze the bookings or sales for the region and, subsequently, selectively drill down into the details of any underperforming region. Another key difference is that data warehouse data is historical and, therefore, time dependent. Its data elements need to have time associated with them, which is part of the key for every record in the database.

Data warehouse tables are very large, contain redundant data, and need to be refreshed periodically from multiple sources. Data warehouses are optimized for fast query processing and access is on an ad hoc basis, rather than through a predefined method.

53 What differentiates databases used by OLTP from data warehouse systems?

The design and operational characteristics of OLTP and data warehouses are very different, as shown in Table 2:

TABLE 2 Comparing Databases

Data Warehouse (DWH)	Traditional Database (OLTP)
Used for data retrieval and analysis	Used to run daily business transactions
Integrated data	Application-specific data
Historical and descriptive data	Current, changing, and incomplete data
Organized by subject	Organized for performance
Nonvolatile data	Constantly changing data
Relational database structure	Relational database structure
Redundant data	Normalized data
Multidimensional data model	Normalized data model
Fewer but larger tables	Larger but fewer tables
Permits drill-down and slice and dice capabilities	Does not allow slicing and dicing
Restructured transaction data for analyzing the business	Detailed transaction data for running the business
Transaction data as well as summarized and derived data	Raw transaction data; could contain some derived data
Contains data about data (metadata)	Contains only data
Optimized for query processing and flexible analysis	Optimized for speed, performance, reliability, data integrity, and security
Queries are unplanned and cannot be easily or quickly optimized	Queries are predefined, small, and can be optimized
Time element is contained in key structure	Time element might or might not be contained in key structure

54 Why are different databases required for data warehouses and OLTP systems?

The performance and features of OLTP and data warehouse databases are quite different because of their unique functional requirements, which require their design and operational characteristics to be very different, as shown in Table 2. Hence, different databases are required to be used for the OLTP system and the data warehouse.

55 How is data stored in data warehouses?

There are two main methods for storing data warehouse data. In the first method, which adheres to database normalization rules to some extent, database tables are grouped together by subject areas, which are constructed based on how the business is run. For example, the subject areas can be bookings, billings, backlog, sales, revenue, and costs, among others. In the second method—the dimensional approach—data is structured into "facts" and "dimensions," which is explained in more detail in chapter 7 of this book.

56 What is the benefit of denormalization?

A normalized transaction database limits the queries that can be run against it, because they can severely impact its performance. Denormalization creates redundant data, in very large tables, that reduces or eliminates the requirement to join multiple tables when a query is run. It provides the flexibility for addressing reporting requirements that are ad hoc and unplanned. Although this technique is suitable for a data warehouse, it is not appropriate for a transaction database, which emphasizes performance over redundancy.

CHAPTER 7

STAR SCHEMA

57 What is a star schema?

A star schema, which is the most-widely used method for designing data warehouse databases, implements a multidimensional model in a relational database. It contains two types of tables, fact and dimension, which are described comprehensively in a subsequent chapter. The schema takes its name from the star-like arrangement of entities, in which a central fact table is surrounded by dimension tables. Each dimension corresponds to a single table. Dimension tables are related to the fact table through keys. They are used to select rows from the fact table.

The star schema is not a normalized model, because its dimension tables are intentionally denormalized, even though it is a relational model. In Figure 2, a single fact table is related, as depicted by the three lines, to three dimension tables through a primary/foreign key relationship.

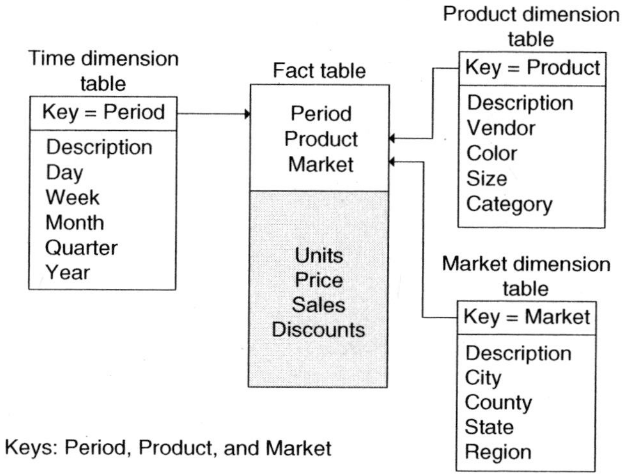

FIGURE 2 Star schema.

58 What are star schema characteristics?

The following characteristics are associated with a star schema:

- Contains two types of tables
  - Fact (major)
  - Dimension (minor)
- One dimension represents one table
- Dimension tables
  - Surround the fact table
  - Are denormalized
  - Are linked to the fact table through unique keys (one per dimension table)
- Every dimension key uniquely identifies a row in the dimension table associated with it
- Fact table's specific row is uniquely identified by the dimension keys
- Uses many entity-relationship diagram (ERD) components
  - Entities
  - Attributes
  - Cardinality
  - Primary keys
  - Relationship connections

59 What are the benefits of the star schema?

The star schema design has many advantages. It favors denormalization for optimizing speed. The denormalization of the time dimension results in a significant reduction in the number of tables that need to be joined when time-based queries are executed. A star schema's performance is superior because one large table (fact table) needs to be joined with a few small tables (dimension tables), resulting in a fast query-response time.

The star schema reflects how business users view data, making it easy for users to comprehend. It is very suitable for query processing, optimizes navigation, makes metadata navigation easier for both programmers and end-users, and permits more versatility in the selection of front-end tools.

60 What is the process for creating a star schema?

During a project's requirements-gathering phase, the metrics, dimensions, and attributes required to support the reporting and analysis needs are identified. After they have been compiled, a data modeler/architect analyzes the results. The next step is to create a data model and to design the star schema, fact and dimension tables, and subject areas. A number of factors are evaluated during this design step, including specific business requirements, subject areas required to support the business needs, performance, utilization level, aggregation requirements, refresh schedule, security, and so forth.

61 What is the impact of a poorly designed star schema?

A star schema that is poorly designed can cause many issues for a data warehouse:

- Poor performance
- Inability to scale and support growth
- Reports cannot be designed because of missing attributes, dimensions, or fact table measures
- Report changes are difficult to implement
- Organizational and business changes are difficult to implement or are impractical
- Loading issues
- Fixes are required frequently
- Report navigation is difficult and confusing

62 What is the snowflake schema?

A snowflake schema, which is derived from the star schema, adds a hierarchical structure to the dimension tables. It is more normalized and complex. The snowflake schema can be used when the dimension table has subcategories, or more than one level of dimension tables, and more efficient access is required. In this structure, the dimension table is normalized into multiple tables, which represent a dimensional hierarchy level. This schema improves query performance but requires more maintenance because of the larger number of tables.

CHAPTER 8

DATA WAREHOUSE PROCESS

63 What is the data warehousing process?

Data warehousing is an integrated process, which encompasses a variety of technologies and processes. The basic process involves extracting, manipulating, and moving data from various source systems into a central database, where it is stored and subsequently analyzed. Data warehousing deals with numerous activities that include planning, extraction, transformation, loading, data design and management, database design and implementation, development, implementation, reporting and analytics, security, operation and maintenance, among others.

64 What are the data warehouse process components?

A data warehouse consists of many components, ranging from simple to complex, which can be grouped into three main categories (see Figure 3):

- Acquisition component
  - Interfaces with the source systems from where it imports data into the data warehouse
- Storage component
  - A large physical database that stores data imported into the data warehouse
- Access component
  - Consists of front-end access and query tools that access and analyze data stored in the data warehouse

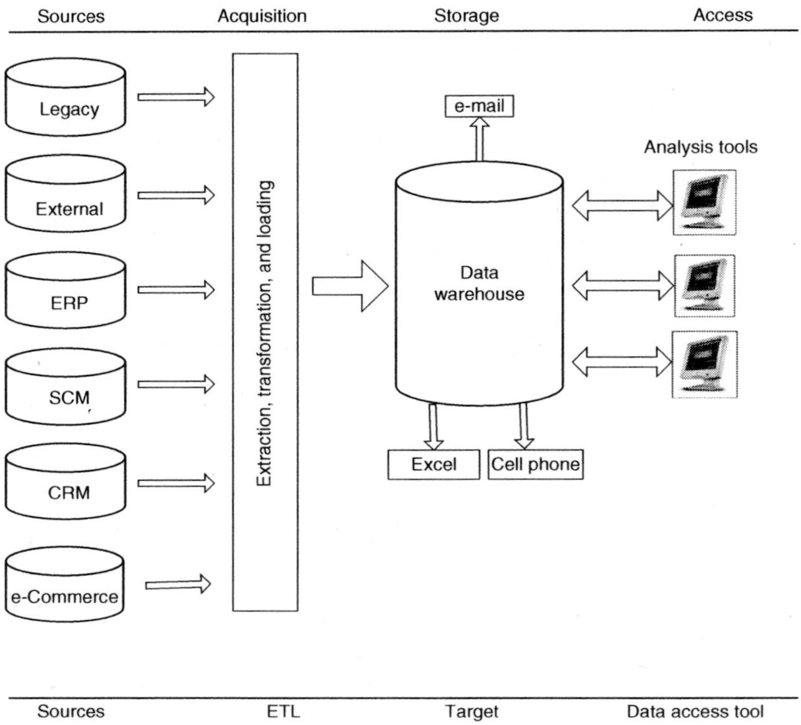

FIGURE 3 Data warehousing process.

65 What is the acquisition component?

The data fed into a data warehouse can originate from many sources, though typically it is imported from the organization's transaction database(s). The sources—of different sizes—can be mainframe files, relational and nonrelational databases, flat files, and others. In the vast majority of cases, the source database is an OLTP system containing current transaction data. In some cases, the source is a non-OLTP database, such as a data warehouse or a data mart. Many companies also use external sources to feed data, such as financial, economic, and weather data, into their data warehouses.

66 Why does source data have to undergo various operations before import?

Most of the data sources, internal and external, cannot meet the data warehouse requirement for imported data to be in a specific format—a layout that supports query processing. The reason for this limitation is that most data sources are formatted for transaction processing—not querying and analysis. Also, imported data is often inconsistent, dirty, and in a nonstandard format. Therefore, before it can be loaded into the data warehouse, source data typically needs to undergo formatting and transformation operations in order to remove inconsistencies and achieve standardization. For example, gender in three source systems might be coded differently: M/F, male/female, and 1/2. Hence, before data from these three sources can be imported into a data warehouse, at least two must be transformed so that consistent data is fed into the data warehouse from all three sources.

67 What is the basic data acquisition process?

After the data to be imported into a data warehouse has been identified, it is physically acquired from the source databases. In this step, called data acquisition, data is extracted from the source(s) and transported to the target database. After it is acquired but before it is loaded into the target, however, it is subjected to some transformations that change its characteristics. The transformations can include restructuring the data, denormalizing the tables, adding new fields and keys, and so on. Before loading, the data can also be subjected to various operations:

- Consolidation (merging various data sets into a single master data set)
- Standardization (of data types and fields)
- Scrubbing (cleaning to remove inconsistencies or inaccuracies)
- Summarization

A variety of commercial tools are available to extract, transform, and load the source data.

68 What is the storage component?

There are two databases associated with a data warehouse:

- Source database – database from where data is imported
- Target database – database into which data is imported and stored

The core component of a data warehouse system is a very large target database. It stores the imported data in an integrated format. In this database, data is structured in a denormalized format in contrast to the normalized structure of the source OLTP databases. The size of a target database can be huge, ranging into the terabyte range and, in some cases, even in the petabyte range.

Although, conceptually, only two databases are required (source and target) for a data warehouse, a third type of database is also used frequently. This is an intermediate database, an ODS, into which source data is loaded and staged before being sent to its final destination—the data warehouse (target database).

In many cases, the ODS is used for regular storage, just as the main data warehouse database, and not just as an intermediate staging database. In such cases, the ODS acts as an important architecture component, which stores data in an OLTP format, against which a query can be executed directly. Whenever required, the data stored in such an ODS can be used for analysis, often in conjunction with the main data warehouse data. A data warehouse system can contain many ODSs.

69 What is the access component?

To access and analyze data stored in a data warehouse, and present it to the users, an access/query component is required. This component can include querying, reporting, and decision-support tools. Such tools, which can include data-mining software, can typically support queries, calculations, what-if analysis, as well as other advanced functions. Most data warehouse users use standard reports and queries. Only a small percentage of data warehouse users create ad hoc and custom reports, which are usually developed by business analysts, power/super users, and IT personnel.

70 Are front-end access tools simple or complex?

The sophistication of the available data-access tools varies significantly. They range from low-end tools, with simple querying capabilities, to high-end tools that can perform sophisticated multidimensional analysis. The simplest tool is MS-Excel, whereas data-mining tools are at the other end of the spectrum. The recent trend has been to Web enable such tools, a feature that provides many benefits. A Web-enabled tool is more versatile and is easy to use; it eliminates the need to install special software on every desktop, provides access through a simple browser, and helps reduce costs because it requires less powerful and expensive hardware.

71 Who can use the front-end access tools?

The front-end tools can be utilized by users at different ends of the skills spectrum and the corporate hierarchies, because the tools are quite versatile and are able to cater to the needs of the diverse data-warehouse-user base.

CHAPTER 9

ARCHITECTURE

72 What should be the foundation for the architecture?

The data warehouse architecture should, ideally, be designed within the context of the enterprise information architecture, which is based on the organization's information requirements that support the strategic goals of the enterprise. The foundation of the enterprise information architecture is the enterprise data architecture, which is a fully normalized enterprise data model. The enterprise technical architecture lays out the vision for the infrastructure, platforms, hardware, and operating systems, as well as plans for other elements.

The business requirements should be used as the foundation for the architecture and, therefore, should be reflected in the architecture and design of the data warehouse. Instead of specific technologies, these business requirements should be used as the basis for the enterprise data model and components. The architecture should be scalable, flexible, and should reflect the need for analytical processing, rather than transaction processing.

The data warehouse architecture drivers are as follows:

- Current infrastructure and systems
- Corporate strategy and politics
- Business and operational plans
- Emerging technologies
- End-user requirements

The data warehouse architecture is typically organized via the following four components (Figure 4):

- Application layer
- Data
- Infrastructure (technology and security)
- Support (including processes and resources)

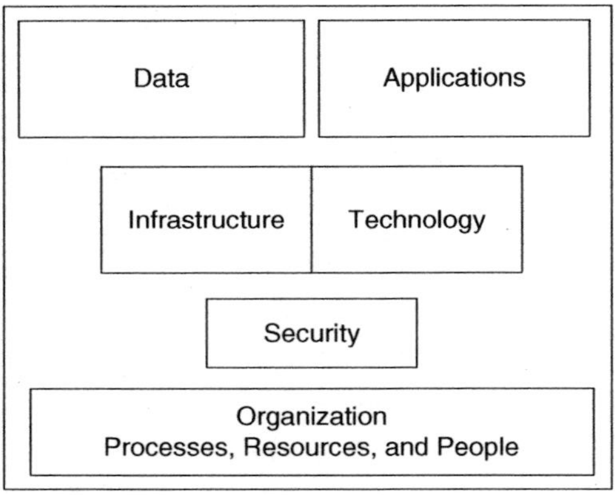

FIGURE 4 Data warehouse architecture components.

The technical architecture of a data warehouse contains many components, including source inputs, ETL, database management system (DBMS), storage, middleware, communication, access, presentation, metadata management, administration, security, to mention a few.

73 What does the architecture have to support?

The primary objective of the architecture is to support the strategic and operational information requirements of the enterprise. It is the structure that must glue together the three main functions of the data warehouse: data acquisition, data storage, and information delivery.

74 Which infrastructure components support the architecture?

There are two basic infrastructure components required to support a data warehouse:

- Physical infrastructure
- Operational infrastructure

The physical infrastructure consists of various components including the server and other hardware, operating system, DBMS, networks, network software, information delivery tools, and access hardware. The operational infrastructure includes the elements needed to implement and operate the data warehouse, which include resources, procedures, support infrastructure, and the like.

75 How is poor architecture manifested?

Many data warehouse implementations fail because the system is built upon a poorly designed architecture. This can be manifested in a number of ways, including deficiencies in schema, data-access method, ETL, network architecture, client/server architecture, and metadata. Creating a data warehouse based on a flawed architecture is a very serious mistake because it is the most difficult—and costly—error to rectify once it has been implemented. Hence, it is imperative that a top-notch data warehouse architect design the overall architecture.

76 What does the data-warehouse-application-and-deployment architecture comprise?

The data-warehouse-application architecture comprises the three components, or layers, that make up an application:

- Presentation (what the user sees—the client-side view)
- Functional logic (underlying business rules)
- Data (physical data storage layer)

77 What functions do the three- and four-tier architectures comprise?

Most data warehouses have been implemented using the three-tier architecture. The first tier (i.e., the server), hosts the data warehouse database and handles data processing. The second tier (i.e., the client), hosts the front-end access tool and handles the presentation component. The third tier, an intermediate tier between the server and the client, is the application tier that supports the functional logic and services.

The four-tier architecture is also available for data warehouse implementations. It is characterized by the addition of an additional Web component—a Web server.

78 What should be avoided when defining the architecture?

A data warehouse should not be designed for a particular technology. Its architecture must be designed before the technology is selected. Failure to design the architecture first can prevent the requirements from being supported by the selected technology, which cannot be easily modified or discarded because of the extremely high costs associated with scrapping or modifying a deployed infrastructure. Because many choices and options are available (many technologies support data warehousing), rarely should any factor force an organization to implement, for its data warehousing needs, a specific technology that is not in sync with its proposed architecture.

79 How can users impact the architecture and capacity?

Data warehouse usage grows exponentially if it is implemented successfully and meets or exceeds the needs of its users. Success manifested through an upsurge in the number of users, however, can create capacity constraints if the system and network are inadequately designed. Hence, a well-designed data warehouse should be able to accommodate growth, should exhibit good performance and avoid slow response times, and should be scalable.

CHAPTER 10

METADATA

80 What is metadata?

Metadata has usually been described as "data about data." It has also been described as the "DNA of the data warehouse" as well as the "data warehouse directory." Metadata is a key element in the data warehouse architecture and is critical for constructing, managing, and using the data warehouse. It provides useful information for locating data stored in a data warehouse. All data about the data, as mapped between the source and target systems, is resident in the metadata. The metadata includes a description of the data warehouse fields and tables, data types, and acceptable value ranges.

81 Who uses metadata?

Metadata can be used by the technical resources, such as IT staff, back-end developers, report developers, business analysts, managers, support staff, and administrators. It can also be useful for super users and power users, who often develop reports and queries. Metadata can also be useful, in some cases, for light and casual users, who may need some details about the reports that they use.

82 What are the benefits of metadata?

Metadata provides useful mapping information, such as where the data came from—legacy systems, files, databases, and fields. It documents relationships between data structures within databases. It also provides information about the data structure—tables and columns as well as their definition and descriptions. It is also the source of information about operations that were applied on data imported into the data warehouse. These include the following:

- Selection criteria
- Filters
- Business rules
- Transformation and integration operations
- Cleansing
- Algorithms used to summarize and derive data

Metadata can provide many additional benefits. For example, it can be used to track the relationship between the data model and the data warehouse, review how the business definitions and calculations changed over time, and provide a history of extracts and changes in data over time. Metadata often resides outside the data warehouse in a database or a formal repository.

83 What are the different types of metadata?

Many metadata types have been described that are usually categorized either by "usage" or by "who uses it." For example, one classification contains two types: business metadata and technical metadata. Business metadata, which is for the business users, provides information about the data, its sources, definitions, and the like, in business terminology. Technical metadata, which defines the objects and processes in the data warehouse, is used by the technical team. Kimball, one of the original data warehousing architects, also refers to a third type of metadata, process metadata, which documents the data warehouse operations. Of the three types of metadata that have been defined, business and technical metadata are commonly referred to as metadata. Figure 5 depicts the relationship between the data warehouse systems and its metadata repository.

Another categorization defines metadata as "structural" or "access." Structural metadata is used to create and maintain the data warehouse. It is based on the data warehouse model that describes data entities as well as their relationships. Access metadata provides the dynamic link between a data warehouse and its associated applications.

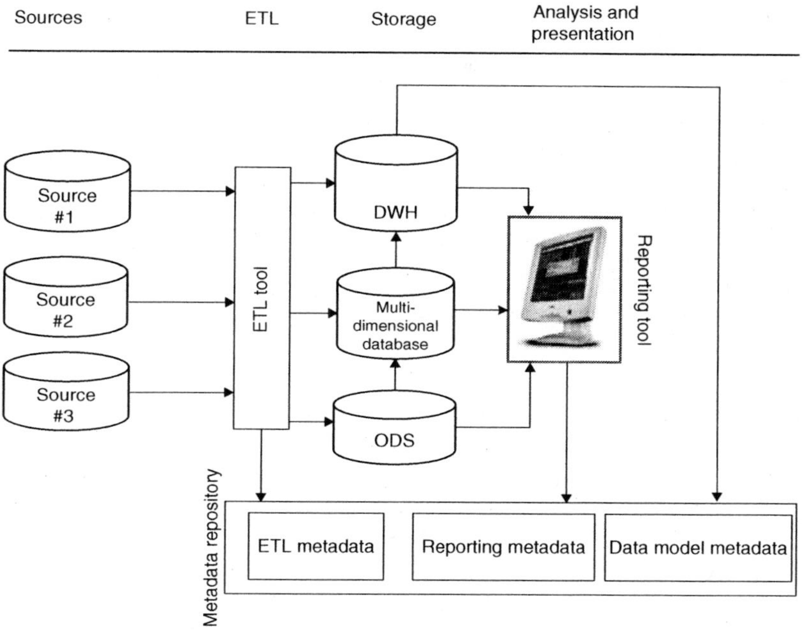

FIGURE 5 Data warehouse metadata repository.

84 Has any metadata standard been defined?

Metadata tools are difficult to select because, at present, there is no universally accepted metadata standard that is being used for data warehouse systems. Even though there have been attempts to achieve such a standard, limited progress has been made until now. Some initial efforts were made to develop metadata standards, by the Meta Data Coalition and the Object Management Group. They had, respectively, released two standards, Open Information Model (OIM) and Common Warehouse Metamodel (CWM), which incorporated technologies such as Unified Modeling Language (UML), Extensible Markup Language (XML), and Simple Object Access Protocol (SOAP).

In 2000, the merger of these two organizations resulted in the creation of the Object Management Group (OMG). It has published various standards, including the Meta-Object Facility (MOF) and the XML Metadata Interchange (XMI). However, there are a limited number of tools that currently leverage these standards.

CHAPTER 11

SOURCE DATA

85 How is a data warehouse populated with data?

A data warehouse is populated with data from its source systems, which can be internal as well as external. This data is imported via the data migration process. In many cases, it is also required to undergo data conversion prior to being loaded into the target data warehouse system. The initial load is massive, because data from a 2- to 3-year period or longer is brought in from the source systems. Later on, after the data warehouse becomes operational, the routine loads are incremental, and might or might not need conversion, depending on the design.

86 How much data is loaded?

Source data is initially fed into a data warehouse in a massive upload. Subsequently, additional new data is loaded with a frequency ranging from once a day to real-time, depending on the organization's requirements. Another type of upload is in the reverse direction. In this procedure, the data warehouse is converted into a source system and feeds data to another data warehouse, a data mart, or a legacy system.

87 What are the desired characteristics of imported data?

Data warehouse data must meet the highest quality standards. The desired characteristics of the data to be imported into a data warehouse are as follows:

- Clean
- Consistent
- Accurate

- Complete
- Reliable
- Relevant
- Current
- Timely

Before data is imported, it must be checked and validated to ensure that it is properly structured, and that it is accurate and complete. If the data is inaccurate and unreliable, it will lose its credibility and, consequently, be ignored by the users. If inaccurate data is used for decision making, the quality of decisions can be compromised and serious consequences can be expected.

Concrete steps need to be taken to ensure data quality. The data cleanup process must start at the source data, which often requires complex cleaning. Failure to do so can have very negative repercussions, including project failure, interruption in business operations, and incorrect reports and analyses.

88 How are data sources identified and selected?

The first step in the data migration process is the identification of the source systems that will feed data into the data warehouse. Because data duplication is a common problem, and many data elements can be found in multiple data sources, the source systems will need to be analyzed to determine the best source for importing data. Such a source and its data elements must be reliable and accurate. They must preferably be in the required format or need minimum transformation for import into the data warehouse. To perform the source identification task, considerable time and effort are usually required because of the differences and possible anomalies that can exist among the various source databases.

89 Why should detailed and external data be imported?

It is a mistake to use summarized data as the foundation of a data warehouse because, in many cases, real value is to be found in the detailed transaction data. Besides limiting flexibility, lack of detailed data restricts the types of analyses that can be performed. To maximize the benefits of a data warehouse, all potentially beneficial external and internal data sources should be utilized. External data can be very useful and should not be ruled out.

90 Why should historical data be imported?

The more data that a data warehouse contains, both historical and operational, the more useful it can be to its users. The availability of historical data can enable meaningful trending and comparisons. Although it is beneficial to import historical data, the data to be imported should be relevant and cost-effective.

91 What are the common problems associated with source data?

Source data is frequently "dirty" and inconsistent. It is common for different data sources within the same organization to identify the same customer in multiple ways. For example, IBM might show up in different sources as "IBM," "International Business Machines," or "IBM Global Services." Therefore, any report, query, summation, or analysis performed on a system containing these three variations can return inaccurate results.

The range of problems commonly encountered covers a wide spectrum, including the following:

- Field data not matching the field description
- Data files from disparate sources in differing formats
- Inconsistent spelling of name in different systems
- Address variation across sources
- Multiple names located in the same field
- Name and address in the same field
- Inconsistent use of special characters
- Zip codes missing from addresses
- Area codes missing from phone numbers

- Inconsistent spacing
- Truncated data

92 What are legacy source data issues?

The following are common issues associated with data imported from source systems, especially legacy systems:

- Inaccuracy and poor quality of data in legacy systems
- Files extracted from multiple sources storing data in different formats
- Field descriptions not matching the data values or following business rules
- Considerable data granularity variation in the source databases
- Mapping lacking simplicity or straightforwardness because of data structure and storage formats varying considerably across systems
- Difficulty in matching and relating entities, creating issues for presenting consolidated views
- Business entities being represented in disparate ways, complicating the task of consolidation

93 What is the cost of importing source data?

It is estimated that 50%–75% of the time required to build a data warehouse is spent on ETL, which includes the following tasks:

- Analyzing the data
- Extracting data from the sources
- Conditioning and transforming source data for meeting the requirements (technical and business)
- Loading the data

Despite the availability of many ETL tools with automated functions, the data migration task still requires considerable manual effort. The total effort expended for the overall ETL task can be significantly higher if custom ETL programs are utilized. Some of the data warehouse database vendors provide embedded ETL tools, which simplify the data migration task, because they can leverage the predefined mappings that are provided with those tools.

CHAPTER 12

DATA CONVERSION AND MIGRATION

94 What is data conversion?

Data conversion refers to the process of converting data from one format into another. For example, if data from a mainframe or flat files is required to be loaded into a data warehouse's relational database, it will need conversion because of differences in storage types and data structures, as well as variations in data encoding across computer systems. Operating system variations also come into play, as they operate on different standards for data and file handling. Additionally, computer programs handle data in different ways. Data conversions can be simple or very complex, which can impact the degree of effort and cost involved in the extraction effort.

95 How is data converted?

There exist many techniques that are used for converting data. In general, a file is read, interpreted, converted, and output into a new file. The conversion can be performed using data conversion programs or custom computer programs developed in-house. A number of third-party tools are available for this purpose.

96 What is data migration?

Data migration is the process of transferring data from an existing system to a new system, such as a data warehouse. The migration is implemented using custom programs, or third-party tools, that transfer the data automatically, based on predefined rules. The method selected depends on many variables such as the systems involved, data volume and complexity, data quality, cost, and availability of resources.

In data warehousing, the data migration process is a very complicated task because the number, type, and quality of the data sources vary significantly. It requires considerable effort because the source data and processes need to be analyzed thoroughly before a decision can be made on how to implement the data migration task.

97 What is involved in the data migration process?

There are four basic steps that need to be performed for data migration:

- Analyzing source system and determining its data structure
- Determining data structure of the new system, the data warehouse
- Mapping fields between the two systems; identifying common fields in the old and new systems in order that data, when moved from the source system, will arrive in the proper location in the data warehouse
- Defining migration process so that the actual import process, in which the data is extracted and then loaded, is automated

98 What are the differences between data migration and data integration?

Data migration refers to the task that involves moving data from one environment or source system to another environment or system. This is typically implemented as a project, and, in many cases, the source system is retired after the data migration. On the other hand, data integration is a process, based on data flows within different data sources and applications, which provides users with a unified view of the data. It has been gaining popularity in recent years as data volumes have exploded and the need to share data internally and with partners has increased dramatically.

99 What is the environment that requires data migration?

Data migration is driven by four primary reasons:

- Storage migration
- Database migration
- Application migration
- Business process migration

The environment in which the migration has to be performed in each of these cases—which include data warehouse migration—is complex and includes the following characteristics:

- Multiple data sources
- Varying data quality
- Inconsistent nomenclature and definitions
- Inconsistent data
- Data models that vary across the databases
- Consolidation requirements across nonstandard aging legacy systems
- Lack of skilled legacy IT resources

100 Why is data migration a complex task?

The data migration task is very complicated because the number, type, and quality of the sources feeding the data warehouse can vary significantly. The migration requires considerable effort because the source data and processes need to be analyzed comprehensively before the extraction process can be designed and the data loaded. In conventional data warehouse implementations, 75% of the build time is spent on the following tasks:

- Extracting data from the sources
- Conditioning and transforming source data for meeting the technical and business requirements
- Loading the data into the data warehouse

The task of populating a data warehouse system with data from multiple inconsistent sources is very challenging and requires a significant investment of time and resources. Migrating data from these complex systems is a challenge that, if not well managed, can lead to data quality issues or project delays. In some cases, it can even cause a project to fail.

101 How much data should be migrated?

The amount of data to be imported is usually driven by the business requirements. Typically, the business wants the maximum volume of data, extending over many years, to be imported. On the other hand, IT wants to minimize the data to be imported due to the ETL effort involved, which can be very time consuming and expensive, as well as the effort required to clean and validate the additional data to be imported. The final decision regarding the period for which data is to be imported is usually a compromise between overburdening IT and fulfilling the requirements of the business.

Importing insufficient data into the data warehouse can limit the analyses that can be performed. Because highly granular data allows maximum analytical versatility, import of transaction data should be maximized even though it significantly increases data volumes. In general, the usefulness and versatility of a data warehouse increases as the data stored in it increases. However, storing too much data, especially if it is irrelevant, can have a negative impact because it will require extra effort for the ETL and data validation tasks. Therefore, the amount and type of data to be selected for import should be limited to whatever is required to help the users to be effective and efficient.

102 Can data migration be automated?

The initial data load into a data warehouse is based on very large data volumes. Even though data marts are relatively smaller, their initial data-load volumes can also be quite large. Subsequently, new data needs to be introduced, periodically, to refresh and update a data warehouse and/or data marts. For this purpose, predefined extraction, mapping, and loading routines are used to feed data from the source systems at predefined frequencies. As required, such routines can be automated to extract source data and move it into the data warehouse, while maintaining data integrity during the transfer, based on predefined business rules. There are many software tools that can be used to automate data migration to a considerable degree.

103 What are the challenges in selecting a data migration tool?

Many third-party software tools are available for data migration. Such products, which are quite versatile, can validate names and addresses when multiple sources are being consolidated, rectify errors in the data elements, create new data in the format required by the data warehouse, and so forth. The challenge is to select an appropriate tool that can meet the conflicting requirements of ease of use, quality, speed, scalability, cost, application specifications, and future usage.

104 Why is the migration effort frequently underestimated?

Underestimating the effort and difficulties associated with migrating data from multiple sources into the data warehouse is a widespread problem for many reasons. The most common reason is that the data quality is frequently far worse than expected, which can cause many problems and delay a critical task—validating the imported data. Also, designing the ETL processes for extracting data from multiple courses and loading them into a single target is one of the most difficult, challenging, and costly tasks in a data warehouse project.

105 How can data migration challenges be reduced?

Data migration problems can be avoided:

- By not having unrealistic data quality expectations
- By being prepared to find very dirty data
- By not underestimating the task effort and duration

- By building contingency into the project plan
- By not taking shortcuts in the ETL process—lack of thoroughness can impact data warehouse integrity

These challenges and risks can also be mitigated, to some extent, by using the available state-of-the-art tools for data transformation, cleansing, capturing, and loading.

CHAPTER 13

DATA QUALITY

106 What is data quality?

Data quality is an indicator of the effectiveness and reliability of data. The data in a data warehouse should be able to meet the requirements for which it is meant to be used. In other words, data should be accurate, complete, relevant, trusted, and timely. This applies to the overall system, not just individual data fields.

107 What are the characteristics of good data quality?

There are literally scores of attributes that have been used to define quality data. The following is a list of characteristics that are frequently identified and associated with good quality data:

- Accuracy
- Completeness
- Conformity
- Consistency
- Integrity
- Timeliness and availability
- Auditability
- Relevance
- Understood and trusted by users
- Lack of duplication
- Presentation quality

108 What are the common reasons for data quality problems?

There are many causes of data quality problems—technical and non-technical:

- Business changes (mergers and acquisitions)
- Organizational restructuring
- Changing business rules
- Consolidations
- Inadequate control/management of database and/or applications
- Lack of ownership
- Lack of control
- Integration of systems/applications over time
- Application changes
- Process changes
- Workarounds
- Lack of standards
- Violation of business rules
- Data entry errors
- Fields populated incorrectly
- Data purging
- Data and system conversions over time
- Poor design
- ETL errors
- Lack of accountability for data quality
- Lack of validity checks in applications
- Deficient procedures

109 What are common types of data quality problems?

The types of data quality problems that are very common include, to mention a few, missing data, wrong data type, wrong data values in field, duplicate data, dummy values, truncated values, inconsistent values, missing or incorrect relationships, and incompatible hierarchies.

110 What benefits can be achieved by improving data quality?

There are many benefits associated with improved data quality in a data warehouse environment:

- Improved confidence
- Higher reliability
- Reduced risk
- Reduced maintenance
- Higher productivity
- Customer satisfaction
- Less time required for reconciliation
- Improvement toward goal of "one version of the truth"

111 Can poor data quality cause serious issues?

Many data warehouse implementations have faced problems, including very serious ones, when the data was not cleaned before import or validated after loading. Some of the issues associated with poor data quality are inaccurate or inconsistent reports, lack of confidence in the data warehouse, corrupted data, high maintenance costs, data redundancy, legal and compliance issues, and flawed decision making.

112 What is data cleansing?

Before source data is acquired and loaded into the target database, it is cleansed or scrubbed in order to remove errors that are commonly found in the source systems. This task can involve a number of steps such as:

- Identifying redundant data
- Correcting or deleting inaccurate or corrupt records
- Rectifying erroneous values in fields
- Populating fields with missing values
- Standardizing the format

The techniques used include parsing, data transformation, elimination of duplicates, and statistical methods. There is a direct relationship between the amount of effort expended in data cleansing and the number of loading errors encountered when data is moved from the source to the target database. In general, the more thorough the data-cleansing effort is, the lower the number of errors.

113 How can data quality be improved?

There are many ways in which data quality can be improved:

- Highlighting the importance of data quality
- Involving management
- Developing data standards and procedures
- Initiating performance evaluation criteria
- Assigning data ownership
- Using appropriate tools and techniques
- Providing training
- Involving the business with IT
- Auditing data
- Using a methodology that is data driven
- Using new data-oriented technologies such as master data management (MDM)

114 How can MDM help improve data quality?

MDM is a management, rather than maintenance, tool. Instead of maintaining data in each transaction system, MDM manages it at the enterprise level, which enables a consistent view of data and performance across the enterprise. The benefits of MDM in a business intelligence environment are as follows:

- Improves data governance of master data entities
- Identifies data quality issues through data profiling
- Identifies costs associated with dirty data
- Identifies cost benefits that can result if data issues are fixed
- Improves business insight
- Provides a mechanism and tool for fixing data issues
- Improves efficiency through cost reduction, simplification of master data processes, and improved business process control
- Reduces manual work for reconciliation and fixes, and increases level of automation
- Optimizes services
- Improves analysis
- Enables faster analysis
- Reduces risk
- Improves regulatory compliance
- Increases confidence
- Improves global capabilities

115 What are the various types of data-cleansing tools?

There are two main categories of data-cleansing tools:

- Data error discovery tools – focus on identifying inaccurate and inconsistent data
- Data correction tools – focus on correcting corrupted data

There are tools available in both categories. Although some might excel in just one of the categories, many of them perform some functions in both categories.

116 What is data validation?

Because the data loaded into a data warehouse can be defective, it is required to undergo data validation, which refers to the checking of imported data to ensure that it is accurate, consistent, complete, and ready to be used. This is an important task that must be carried out to reduce potential serious problems after the data warehouse goes live. The type and extent of verification performed varies from implementation to implementation.

117 Are adequate resources allocated to data cleanup and validation tasks?

A considerable amount of effort is required to clean source data before it is introduced into the data warehouse. However, this task is frequently neglected or underestimated and, therefore, insufficient resources are allocated for the cleanup and validation task. This often creates problems during the implementation phase as well as during operations. In many cases, failure to address this task adequately has caused serious reliability and operational problems after the data warehouse went live because queries, based on incorrect data, produced inconsistent and unreliable results.

CHAPTER 14

ETL PROCESS

118 What are the main ETL components?

The data acquisition process is grouped into three main components:

- Extraction
    - Involves pulling data from the source system(s)
- Transformation
    - Involves subjecting the data to a number of operations before importing it
- Loading
    - Involves physically placing extracted and transformed data into the target database

119 What is the role and importance of the ETL process?

An extremely important and difficult task in building a data warehouse involves extracting, transforming, and loading huge volumes of data stored in a variety of disparate source systems. The ETL process is the core data warehouse process, whose design and development is very expensive. It can easily consume 50%–75% of the data warehouse project's budget.

The ETL task is very time consuming because it requires cleaning and integrating data of significantly varying quality that is stored in many systems and formats. Hence, it is critical that the ETL task be given the importance that it deserves. It should be implemented with adequate resources by skilled and experienced IT personnel. It needs to be accomplished through a well-designed architecture that is reliable, scalable, and supports the extraction, transformation, and loading of the data elements that need to be fed into the data warehouse.

120 What are ETL challenges?

The ETL process faces numerous challenges, many of which can derail a project or impact business operations:

- Complex environments that need to be integrated
- Multiple sources with different architectures and structures
- Source data in incompatible formats
- Poor data quality
- Poor data model design
- Complex transformation and cleansing rules
- Conflicting business definitions and rules
- Historical data conversion issues
- Impact of historical organizational changes
- Lack of procedures for resolving inconsistencies
- Obsolete and/or incompatible tools and/or technologies
- Lack of attention to data validation
- Time-consuming procedures
- Changes in requirements during development, leading to continual ETL changes
- Insufficient resources for ETL development
- Inadequate ETL developer skills

121 How long does the ETL process take?

Of all the data warehouse implementation tasks, the extraction, transformation, and loading process consumes the most significant amount of time. The actual duration depends on the overall scope and duration of the project. Typically, this task can take up to 50% of the total project cycle. However, this can be considerably less if the project requires minimal customization and, where available, out-of-the box data marts and/or reports/dashboards are utilized.

122 What is involved in extraction (E)?

In this step, data is extracted from the source systems. The objective is to convert the data, which could be in different formats (such as VSAM, ISAM, relational, and flat files) into a single format that is ready for transformation processing. The extracted data is parsed to check whether it conforms to a pattern or a specific structure. The techniques for performing data extraction vary and are influenced by many factors, including type and structure of source data, availability of tools, extraction frequency, and exception handling.

123 What is involved in transformation (T)?

Source data is subjected to a number of operations that prepare it for import into the data warehouse (target database). To perform this task, integration and transformation programs are used. These programs apply business rules or functions to the extracted data in order to reformat, recalculate, modify the structure and data elements, and add time elements. They are also used to perform calculations and a variety of other tasks, such as summarization and denormalization.

In a few cases, very little or no manipulation is required. However, in many cases, a range of operations might be required on some or all of the data. Some of the operations include filtering, joining, translating values, encoding, sorting, aggregating, calculating a new derived value, and pivoting (transposing).

124 What is involved in loading (L)?

The loading process involves physically moving extracted and transformed data into the target database. Initially, a large volume of data is loaded into the data warehouse. Subsequently, an extraction procedure loads fresh data periodically, based on business rules and a predetermined frequency. The loading process and volume can vary according to business requirements. For example, some functional areas could require data to be added daily, whereas some will perhaps require real-time or near real-time data loading. Requirements can also vary with regard to the period for which the data, detailed or aggregate, needs to be made available, which, consequently, influences the ETL process and frequency.

The amount of data to be loaded determines the time it takes for the extraction and loading process. Depending on the data volume, the loading time can vary from a few minutes to many hours. The loading time can also impact the analysis. For example, if the loading takes four hours, then data will not be available for any prior four-hour period. Therefore, it will not be possible to run reports for any prior four-hour period. To avoid performance impact issues, most data loading is done after normal working hours, usually at night.

According to a 2009 The Data Warehouse Institute (TDWI) survey, only 17% of respondents reported the use of real-time functionality in their data warehouses (*http://tdwi.org/newsletters/experts-di/2010/09/092310.aspx*). However, 92% indicated that they expected to use real-time functionality within three years. Therefore, the ETL process will face even greater challenges in the future, as it tries to provide data within a time frame that does not provide much margin for extraction and loading errors to be rectified.

125 What ETL operations are applied to source data?

All source data might need to undergo some or all of the following operations in the data warehousing process:

- Mapping
- Cleaning
- Restructuring and reformatting
- Recalculation
- Selecting/filtering
- Summarization
- Validation
- Reconciliation

There are additional ETL tasks as well:

- Merge processing
  - When multiple data sources are used
- Purge processing
  - When some filtering rules are applied to weed out unwanted data
- Staging
  - When source data needs to be placed in an intermediate storage location before it is read by, and imported into, the data warehouse
- Back flushing
  - If clean validated data warehouse data is to be fed back to the source system(s)

126 What is involved in ETL testing?

ETL testing, which is performed by the development team, involves the testing of various processes, including data extraction, transformation, data cleansing, and loading. Following are the essential elements required for testing the ETL process:

- Completeness
  - Confirms that all data is loaded as expected
- Transformation
  - Confirms that all data is accurately transformed, as per business rules and criteria
- Data quality
  - Validation, filtering, substitutions, and other operations performed are as expected; ensures that the ETL application rejects correctly, substitutes default values, and corrects, ignores, and reports invalid data

- Scalability
  - Is able to scale as load volumes increase and queries demand more data
- Performance
  - Performance is acceptable and data loading is completed within acceptable time windows

The testing is absolutely essential because failure, at a later stage, can be far more expensive and disruptive to the business.

127 What are the specific tasks involved in ETL testing?

Following are some of the tasks that are performed during ETL testing:

- Completeness
  - Involves multiple subtasks including performing full and incremental loads, verifying that new records have been added as expected, validating loading (all records, fields, and content of each field), counting volumes, comparing unique values of key fields between source data and data loaded into the warehouse, and validating that no truncation occurs at any step in the process
- Transformation
  - Involves validating that data is transformed correctly, based on business rules, either manually or through an automated process, comparing range and distribution of values in each field between source and target data, validating correct processing of ETL-generated fields such as surrogate keys, validating parent-to-child relationships in the data, etc.
- Data quality
  - Involves validating how the ETL system handles data rejection, correction, and notification without modifying data

- Performance
  - Points out any potential weaknesses in the ETL design, such as reading a file multiple times or creating unnecessary intermediate files. Tasks performed include comparing ETL loading times to loads performed with a smaller amount of data for anticipating scalability issues; comparing the ETL processing times, component by component, to point out any areas of weakness; monitoring the timing of the reject process; determining how large volumes of rejected data are handled; performing simple and multiple join queries to validate the query performance on large database volumes, etc.

CHAPTER 15

ETL ISSUES, TOOLS, AND ELT

128 What are the potential problems and challenges of ETL?

The ETL task can face many problems due to a variety of reasons:

- Unanticipated complexity
- Conflicting business rules
- Changing business requirements
- Frequent changes in design
- Flawed or inadequate design
- Incorrect mapping
- Longer loading times than designed
- Dirtier data than expected
- Insufficient development time
- Problems due to lack of validation
- Flawed testing process
- Inadequate tools
- Inferior developer skills
- Infrastructure issues

129 Why is the ETL task often underestimated?

The ETL task is the most difficult and labor-intensive activity in the data warehouse project. It is frequently underestimated, leading to cost overruns and project delays. The scope of this task is often underestimated for the following common reasons:

- Incorrect assumption about data quality
- Unanticipated complexity of design
- Unanticipated complexity of business logic
- Incorrect estimation of programming effort
- Unrealistic expectations about ETL tool capabilities
- Higher-than-expected complexity in extracting and loading data from numerous sources
- Additional validation effort required for larger-than-expected data volumes
- Lack of guidance from subject matter experts

130 How are ETL tasks handled?

ETL tasks are handled by a variety of tools. Some of them, such as file transfer programs, are fairly simple. However, some tools, such as those used for data transformation, can be fairly complex and are able to perform the following functions:

- Automate data extraction from multiple sources
- Map sources to the target database
- Transform and/or manipulate data
- Load data into the data warehouse

Technologies used in the ETL process include ASCII, XML, HTML, DB Connect, IDoc, BAPI, and SOAP.

131 What are the common tasks performed by ETL tools?

Many tools, from a number of vendors, are available for executing ETL tasks. There are three primary functions that ETL tools are required to accomplish:

- Read data from a source, such as a relational database table, flat file, or other

- Manipulate data (filter, modify, or enhance), based on specific rules
- Write resulting data to the target database

There are many intermediate and post-loading steps, during and after the three primary ETL operations, including building reference data, performing validation, cleaning, checking integrity, building aggregates, staging, archiving, and purging.

Specific tasks that an ETL tool might be required to perform include the following:

- Converting data
    - Changing the incoming source data into a unified format and definition
- Deriving data
    - Applying mathematical formulae to fields in order to create brand-new fields
- Filtering data
    - Screening unwanted data from source data files before moving it to the data warehouse
- Integrating data
    - Merging files from different databases and platforms
- Summarizing data
    - Combining tables
- Selecting data
    - Selecting and loading data based on triggers

132 What are desired features of ETL tools?

As users clamor for complete solutions, vendors are forced to provide more functionality and reliability. Many database vendors now include several desirable ETL features and functions in their products:

- Richness of features and functions—should include both transformation and cleansing features

- Ability to handle greater complexity of mappings and transformations
- Ability to read various file formats
- Ability to read directly from the source
- Back-end data management and processing, including metadata management
- Ability to handle real-time, or near real-time, data for ever-tightening batch-processing schedules
- Improved throughput and scalability for handling rising data volumes, even as batch-processing timeframes become narrower
- Ability to handle greater numbers and varieties of data sources (XML, HTML, etc.)
- Improved capability for capturing changes and updates
- Easy to use—for loading and/or updating
- Provide metadata support
- Ability to communicate with different relational databases
- Improved administration

ETL tools should be selected carefully, based on the unique needs of each implementation. Selection of an inappropriate tool can cause many problems.

133 What types of ETL tools are available?

The functionality of the available ETL tools varies considerably and their prices can range from minimal (some are even free) to hundreds of thousands of dollars. At the lower end are simple data migration tools whose functionality is limited to extraction and loading. However, the more versatile tools are very sophisticated and can perform many tasks such as enabling transformations, handling a wide range of input formats and sources, and so forth. In general, the tools fit into three main categories:

- Data transformation engines
- Code generators
- Data capture through replication

134 What are the ETL tool selection criteria?

The ETL tool to be used must, first and foremost, be appropriate for the environment in which it is to be used. It should support the basic functions required—transformation and cleansing. The desired and/or required ETL features for a particular implementation should be used as the criteria for selecting the tool. Additionally, business factors that come into play include cost, reliability, scalability, vendor reputation, and availability of resources with the skills to use the product effectively. In some situations, it will not make sense to purchase a third-party tool, which can be very expensive and difficult to use. If the data transformation is extremely complex, for example, it might be better to develop in-house custom programs for the ETL process.

135 Who are the leading providers of ETL tools?

The following is a list of well-known ETL tool vendors:

- Informatica® (PowerCenter)
- IBM (InfoSphere Information Server, DataStage)
- Ab Initio
- SAP Business Objects (Data Integrator/Data Services)
- Microsoft (SQL Server Integration Services)
- Oracle Data Integrator (ODI)
- Oracle Warehouse Builder (OWB)
- SAP (Sybase® ETL)
- SAS (SAP Enterprise Data Integration Server)
- Adeptia® (Adeptia ETL Suite)
- DB Software Laboratory® (Advanced ETL Processor)
- Others include Syncsort®, ETI®, iWay Software®, and Open Text®

The following vendors provide open-source ETL tools:

- Pentaho® (Pentaho Data Integration)
- Jaspersoft® (Jaspersoft ETL)

- Talend® (Data Integration)
- Clover® (CloverETL)

136 What are the leading ETL frameworks?

There are numerous proprietary ETL frameworks. Among the well-known vendors in this category are IBM, Informatica, Oracle, Ab Initio, SAP Business Objects, Information Builders, SAS, Microsoft, Pervasive®, Digital Fuel®, HiT Software®, Altova®, and Embarcadero™. The open-source framework vendors include Pentaho, Talend, Jitterbit, RapidMiner, Clover, Apatar, Enhydra, and Scriptella®. Freeware ETL frameworks are also provided by some vendors, including Jaspersoft.

137 What is the impact of parallel processing on ETL?

The implementation of parallel-processing technology, which involves simultaneous processing by two processors, has helped improve the performance of ETL processing, especially where huge data volumes are involved. There are three main methods for implementing this technology:

- Data (splits a data file into smaller ones)
- Pipeline (enables the execution of several components on the same field)
- Component (runs multiple processes on different data streams on the same job)

138 How can ETL performance be improved?

The ETL process that is often the slowest is in the database load phase, during which the lack of speed can be attributed to indexing, concurrency, and data integrity. Therefore, that is an area where many performance improvement measures are being targeted. There are several techniques employed to improve performance:

- Partitioning
- Indexing

- Performing validation in the ETL layer before loading
- Disabling triggers
- Disabling integrity checking (during loading in the target)
- Parallel bulk loading
- Maximizing the use of parallelism

139 What is the ELT process?

In the conventional ETL process, based on business rules, data is transformed in the intermediate step and is then loaded into the final destination—the target database. A variation of the ETL process is the ELT process—**e**xtraction, **l**oading, and **t**ransformation. In the ELT process, data is first extracted and then loaded directly into the data warehouse database. The transformations, if required, are applied in the third step—only after the data has been loaded into the database.

CHAPTER 16

DATA STORAGE

140 How much data storage is required?

The storage requirements are driven by the business requirements, such as the period of time encompassed by the data that has to be made available in the data warehouse. For example, storage required for three years of data will be quite different compared with storage needed for twenty years of historical data.

The individual storage requirements must be calculated for four different storage areas:

- Staging area
  - Depends on a number of factors, such as the specific staging requirements, data volume to be loaded, the number of dimensions and facts to be loaded, etc.
- Main data warehouse
  - The largest storage repository, into which data is loaded from the source systems and retained indefinitely
- Data marts
  - Storage volume depending on requirements of the individual data marts, which can vary considerably
- MDDB database
  - The smaller multidimensional database required for storing OLAP data

141 What are the levels of data stored in data warehouses?

Data is stored in data warehouses for efficient retrieval at three levels:

- Current detailed data
  - Contains transaction-level data
- Lightly summarized data
  - Contains aggregated data, such as revenues by week or by subregion
- Highly summarized data
  - Contains aggregated data, such as revenues by month or by region

Each data level targets a different type of user, ranging from senior executives to operational users. An inventory clerk might need to review the available inventory for a specific item, which requires the availability of detailed data; a Chief Financial Officer (CFO), on the other hand, will typically be more interested in reviewing the performance of a business unit or region, which would require the availability of highly summarized data.

142 What is current detailed data?

The bulk of the data stored in a data warehouse consists of current detailed data, at the lowest level of granularity (detail). It is organized by subject areas and can be stored as detailed or aggregated data. All data items at this level represent snapshots in time. The period for which current detailed data is maintained in a data warehouse varies by organization. Typically, data for two–five years is maintained. However, many organizations store data for very length periods, perhaps as long as 20–25 years. The frequency of data refresh also varies according to business needs. Many organizations perform a daily data load, whereas some prefer to refresh their data in real time.

143 What is lightly summarized data?

Lightly summarized data refers to data that has been rolled up for particular dimensions or attributes. For example, the detailed sales data can be at the daily level, whereas the lightly summarized sales data can be at the monthly level. The requirement for light data summarization in a data warehouse is based on the fact that most users run queries that repeatedly access and analyze the same data elements at a summarized level. Therefore, by storing summarized data, there can be considerable improvement in the performance and storage requirements.

144 What is highly summarized data?

Highly summarized data refers to data that has been rolled up to an even higher level than lightly summarized data. The previous example demonstrates that data can be summarized at a very high level at the annual sales level. The source for highly summarized data can be lightly summarized data or current detailed data. The primary users of highly summarized data are senior executives and strategic users. Their needs are primarily limited to this level, though, if required, they can also access data at a lower level of detail through a drill-down process.

145 What is aggregated data?

Frequently accessed data, such as monthly or annual sales, can be aggregated or accumulated along predefined attributes. For example, car sales data can be aggregated by geography and model by adding the sales dollars for each model within a specific geography. Similarly, overall sales can be cumulated for a week, month, quarter, or year. The data to be stored in an aggregated format is determined by a number of factors, including the frequency and complexity of queries.

146 What are the benefits of aggregating data?

The objective of creating aggregates is to improve performance by reducing the amount of data to be read by a query. When a query is run against aggregated data, the response is faster: less data needs to be accessed, because it is already aggregated. Aggregates enable faster navigation as well as faster query run times. Although aggregates reduce the retrieval cost by reducing the amount of data to be retrieved, there is a cost associated with updating them. The reason is that aggregate rollup is required whenever new data is loaded.

Therefore, dependent aggregates need to be recalculated whenever there are changes in the detailed data, master data, or hierarchies.

147 What is the effect of granularity?

Granularity is an important data warehouse design issue because it affects the volume of data to be stored and the types of queries that can be executed. If data is highly granular, with a very high level of detail, the volume of data to be stored in the warehouse will be huge. A highly granular data warehouse contains very detailed data, which can include every captured transaction, such as individual sales orders and purchase requisitions. A less granular data warehouse contains more highly summarized data, such as total purchase orders issued for each month or total monthly sales by region.

If stored data is very granular, practically any type of query can be run against it. However, if the data is less granular, the types of queries that can be executed will be limited. Usually, senior executives and decision makers require less granular data, because they work with summarized and aggregated data, whereas operational staff requires more granular data. In recent years, however, this distinction has been blurred as the needs and requirements of these two types of users have started to overlap because of changes in the decision-making levels and the empowerment of lower level employees.

148 How can data stored across multiple data marts be accessed?

Sometimes, the data stored in a data mart might not contain all the dimensions or facts that are required by a query. For example, a query cannot be created in the bookings data mart if it requires billing data as well, because the bookings data mart will not contain any billing data.

The solution in such a case is to create a view that will enable access to the two data marts (bookings and billing), without actually joining them physically. For example, in the SAP Business Warehouse (SAP BW) system, this feature is implemented as a MultiProvider. This entity combines data from multiple data marts, however, it does not actually contain any data. When a query is executed, the MultiProvider combines data from its sources and then provides data to the requesting query.

149 What is data archiving?

The data to be archived, and the frequency of its archival, depends on how the data is to be used. If the data warehouse is expected to support operational needs, the requirements could be met by retaining data for a two-year period. However, if the data is to be used for strategic purposes, the retention requirement will be for a considerably longer period, extending for 5–25 years. The archived data granularity might be the same as it is for the current detailed or aggregated data.

150 What are the steps involved in designing a database?

Database design is accomplished in five steps: (1) planning and analysis, (2) conceptual design, (3) logical design, (4) physical design, and (5) implementation. The data model is created in the conceptual design step. It focuses on the data that needs to be stored in the database and how the tables are designed. The functional model focuses on how the data is to be processed, and also on how the queries are to be designed for accessing the database tables.

CHAPTER 17

DATA MODELING

151 What is the objective of data modeling?

The objective of data modeling is to develop an accurate model or graphical representation of the business processes in order to identify data that needs to be captured in the database and the relationships among the data. A data model focuses on the data required and its organization, rather than the operations to be performed on the data. It represents data from the users' perspective and is independent of hardware and software constraints. The star schema is the model of choice to capture data warehouse requirements.

152 Which methodology is used to create a data model?

A widely used methodology for creating a data model is the entity-relationship (E-R) model, which is expressed as an entity-relationship diagram (ERD). It is more suitable for modeling OLTP systems, however. The star schema is the most widely used model for capturing data warehouse requirements.

153 What is a logical data model?

A logical data model graphically depicts the information requirements of a business. It combines the business requirements and data structure—the two most important components of application development. If either one of these is lacking or poorly defined, the result will be an application that fails or is not well accepted.

A logical data model is not a database and is independent of a physical data storage device. While a logical database describes the business requirements, the physical database indicates how they are implemented. A logical data model uses an ERD to put together all the data items or information required to run a business. It includes relationships, cardinality, attributes, and keys. Based on requirements specified by business experts, an ERD is created by a data modeler.

It is imperative that a logical data model be built for every data warehouse project even though it is a labor-intensive and time-consuming activity. A logical data model is the foundation upon which a database for an application is designed. It verifies whether the system will satisfy the business needs. The implementation approach and technique is determined to a large extent by the business requirements and the logical data model.

154 What is a physical data model?

The physical data model is created from the logical data model. Based on the physical data model, the physical database is designed and implemented. The activities in this step include denormalizing the data, selecting keys, creating indexes, and building referential integrity. A well-designed physical data model and database structure ensures system performance and ease of maintenance.

155 What is the dimensional data model?

A dimensional data model, which is widely used in data warehouse systems, meets the requirements for organizing data warehouse data. It consists of a fact table and associated multiple, smaller, dimension tables. The fact table contains the measures (metrics or values), whereas the dimension tables represent the context of the measurements. The basis for their design is the star schema or the snowflake schema.

156 What is the difference between dimensional and E-R modeling?

The E-R model is used for OLTP systems, which desire the removal of data redundancy, data consistency, and efficient data storage. A dimensional model, on the other hand, provides information regarding business processes, enables measures to be viewed and analyzed via several dimensions, and is intuitive for users.

157 Why is it imperative to build a data model?

A data model ensures that data required by the database is represented accurately, completely, and is in a format that can be reviewed by end-users before the design is implemented. It is used to build the physical database because it contains information for defining the tables, keys, triggers, and stored procedures. Without a data model several issues could develop:

- Seriously flawed database design
- Less than optimal efficiency and inadequate performance
- Missed data for critical reports
- Inconsistent results
- Difficult maintenance
- Difficulty in supporting business needs

Skilled data architects who can efficiently design data warehouses are difficult to find, especially for smaller projects. Therefore, data modeling for data warehouses is often flawed or less than optimal because it is not performed by top-notch data modelers or architects.

CHAPTER 18

DATA WAREHOUSE ENGINE AND OPERATING SYSTEM

158 What are the data warehouse infrastructure components?

A data warehouse system consists of a number of hardware components such as servers, workstations (PCs), memory, disk storage units, networks, and so forth. Other components include the database, access tool, operating system, system utilities, procedures, and middleware connectivity tools. The middleware links different data sources to the data warehouse and provides connectivity between the data warehouse and associated components.

159 What role does the data warehouse engine play?

A data warehouse engine, the database, is the core component of a data warehouse. It provides the structure for storing the data required to support the reporting and analysis requirements.

160 What are data warehouse engine requirements?

Some of the engine's technical and business requirements, and factors that determine its selection, include the following:

- Ability to support expected data volumes
- Scalability
- Types of queries

- Flexibility
- Reliability
- Performance
- Cost
- Data loads
- Data-loading time
- Load balancing
- Parallel processing
- Query governor and optimizer
- Replication features
- Hardware and database combination
- Ease of monitoring and administration
- Portability
- Ability to work with various access tools from different vendors
- Application Programming Interfaces (APIs) for tools from leading vendors
- Security
- Metadata management
- Extensibility
- Vendor (reputation and number of database installations)

161 What are database selection criteria?

The following are widely used criteria for selecting databases:

- Data storage (volume) requirements
- Reliability
- Performance
- Scalability

- Types of queries
- Support for SQL
- Metadata management
- Distribution requirement
- Ease of monitoring and administration
- Proprietary or open source
- Vendor support

162 Which are the most popular relational databases?

The following companies provide the leading relational database products:

- Oracle
- IBM
- Microsoft
- Teradata
- Sybase (SAP)

There are three leading open-source products:

- MySQL™
- PostgreSQL®
- SQLite

163 Should an open-source database be considered?

There are advantages as well as disadvantages associated with using an open-source product. Among the critical items to consider are the ability to support the expected data volumes, reliability, and vendor support. As with a proprietary database, it should have the ability to meet the technical and business requirements, which were listed previously.

164 Should a relational or OLAP database be used?

A key data warehouse design decision concerns the database type to be selected: relational database or multidimensional (OLAP) database. The selection of the database type influences the choice of the data access tool, which can be a simple relational query tool, an OLAP tool that provides a multidimensional view of the data, or some other type of specialized decision support tool.

Each database type is characterized by strengths and limitations. Conventional relational databases support the specialized technical requirements of data warehouses such as data extraction and replication, query optimization, and bit-mapped indexes. However, they provide limited support for data cleanup and transformation functions. The strengths of multidimensional databases include the benefits associated with OLAP, as well as fast querying and performance. Their primary drawback is that they are based on a proprietary database solution.

Conventional relational databases provide many of the features that characterize multidimensional databases. In many cases, either type of database can be used. However, for specialized or complex analysis requirements, multidimensional databases are often preferred.

165 What are the popular operating systems?

The most popular operating systems used in data warehouses are the following:

- Unix®
- Windows®
- Linux®

166 What are the desired features of the operating system?

The most desired features of an operating system are listed below:

- Reliability
- Scalability
- Availability

- Security
- Preemptive multitasking
- Multithreaded approach
- Memory protection
- Compatibility with the hardware

167 On which platforms can a data warehouse be implemented?

A data warehouse can be implemented on various platforms including Unix, Windows, Linux, NetWeaver®, and mainframe operating systems. Initially, Unix was used extensively but Windows started making inroads because of its lower cost and ease of administration. The spectrum of platforms includes .Net and Java.

CHAPTER 19

HARDWARE

168 What are the server hardware requirements?

The server is a critical infrastructure component and must be selected very carefully, because the success of the data warehouse depends on it working efficiently. There are several basic requirements a server must supply:

- Superior performance
- Ability to support fast query processing
- Capacity
- Scalability
- Redundancy
- High reliability

169 What is a data warehouse appliance?

A component that includes both integrated hardware and software, that is specifically designed for a data warehouse, is known as a data warehouse appliance. Wikipedia defines it as "a data warehouse appliance consists of an integrated set of servers, storage, operating system(s), DBMS and software specifically pre-installed and pre-optimized for data warehousing" (*http://en.wikipedia.org/wiki/Data_warehouse_appliance*).

170 Which technologies are used by data warehouse appliances?

Data warehouse appliances use massively parallel processors (MPP) technology. The advantages of MPP include superior query performance as well as scalability. This technology was introduced in a data warehouse appliance for the first time by Netezza™ in 2003. Kickfire™, which was acquired by Teradata® in 2010, introduced the dataflow software architecture in 2008.

171 What are the benefits of data warehouse appliances?

Appliances offer a number of benefits:

- Simplicity
- Faster implementation facilitated by out-of-the-box configuration
- Cost reduction
- Scalability
- Performance improvement (parallel performance)
- High availability
- Predictable performance
- Balanced software and hardware
- Simplified one-stop support
- Reduced maintenance/administration requirements

172 Who are the data warehouse appliance vendors?

There are many vendors providing data warehouse appliances, including Netezza (IBM), Teradata, DATAllegro®, Greenplum™ (EMC®), XtremeData™, Kognitio®, ParAccel™, Calpont®, Vertica® (HP), and EXASOL®.

173 What are the selection criteria for the hardware platform and components?

The selection of the hardware platform and components depends on a number of factors:

- Scalability
- Performance

- Storage capacity
- Parallel processing support
- Hardware and database combination
- Compatibility with existing components
- Number of users
- Operating system
- Software
- Complexity of queries
- IT skills and maintenance capabilities
- Budget
- Vendor type and reputation
- Vendor support

Experience has shown that the number of users increases rapidly if they find the data warehouse useful; this usually surprises designers. Underestimating usage and, consequently, hardware requirements creates problems when the number of users increases beyond expectations and queries start to become more complex.

174 What are the software tools used in a data warehouse?

There are many additional tools that are used in data warehouse environments. These include tools for creating reports, multidimensional analyses, dashboards and scorecards, data mining, data modeling, data extraction, data transformation, data cleansing, data loading, middleware, administration, metadata, and schedulers.

175 Why are multiple physical environments required?

The overall development process takes place in multiple environments: development, quality assurance, and production. In many installations, there is an additional environment—training. Each of these environments needs to be set up with the data warehouse processes and tools such as servers, ETL, OLAP, and front-end tools. It is preferable for the different environments to use distinct application and database servers. In other words, the development environment should have its own application server and database server, and the production environment should have its own set of application and database servers.

176 What problems can arise due to inadequate infrastructure planning?

Inadequate infrastructure planning can lead to many post-implementation issues such as performance, capacity, and scalability. It is common for well-designed and successful data warehouses to begin to have network overload and capacity problems shortly after becoming operational. The reason is that a successful data warehouse quickly draws more and more users; such a situation can overwhelm the infrastructure if it is not designed to accommodate a quick and significant rise in usage. When demand soars, it affects both hardware and software. This has caught many organizations by surprise and, consequently, forced them to make expensive, unplanned, hardware and software expenditures at short notice.

177 What are the common causes leading to infrastructure inadequacy?

Selected components and tools can be inadequate or inappropriate for a particular implementation for various reasons:

- Faulty architecture
- Decisions based on previously installed components or available tools
- Incompatibility between components
- Wrong selection criteria
- Accepting vendor claims at face value
- Inadequate testing
- Limited scalability
- Improper sizing

- Lack of network traffic analysis
- Incorrect data volume estimates
- Incompatibility among components and/or tools

178 What can happen if the upgrade strategy is flawed?

The introduction of a new database system in an organization has many associated risks and requires a careful and measured approach. The upgrade of the OLTP system from a legacy nonrelational database to a relational database, or from one relational database to another (from a different vendor), is a complex undertaking and should not overlap the implementation of a data warehouse. The introduction of a relational database, if required for both the OLTP and data warehouse systems, should be phased—not simultaneous. Projects that involve a database upgrade together with a simultaneous data warehouse implementation have been completed successfully, but such attempts are inherently more risky and should be avoided.

CHAPTER 20

DATA ACCESS

179 How is information delivered to users?

After the data has been loaded into the data warehouse, it is delivered as information through multiple mechanisms:

- Reports, which are static reports that are delivered periodically
- Queries, which can range from simple to very complex
- Interactive analysis, which can be a series of ad hoc queries run interactively by advanced users
- Applications, especially Decision Support System (DSS) applications, which run on data fed from a data warehouse

180 Why do data warehouses often fail to meet their full potential?

A data warehouse project is a strategic project that aims to meet the organization's short-term, as well as long-term, reporting and analysis needs. In many cases, data warehouses are developed without a reporting roadmap in place, using an approach that quickly rolls out a few starter reports that the users need, without any long-term plan or consideration. The limitations of such an unplanned approach quickly become apparent.

Another common problem is that data warehouse usage is primarily limited to ad hoc queries and simple reports, and decision support and analytics are neglected. It should be realized that the maximum benefit is typically obtained through strategic analysis of data warehouse data. Data mining, slicing and dicing, and in-depth analysis can produce results that can pay for the data warehouse many times over.

181 What are some objectives that data access tools are required to meet?

The data access and reporting requirements across an organization vary considerably. At the high end are strategic queries that analyze huge amounts of data across multiple dimensions. At the low end are tactical queries, run against limited data that might be updated frequently, which answer operational questions. The requirements of strategic users—the senior executives—are quite different compared with the needs of line managers, front-line workers, and power users. Therefore, an organization's requirements can range from canned status reports, which are most widely used, to complex ad hoc queries that are developed dynamically and interactively by a limited number of users.

182 What types of front-end tools are available?

The most common types of data-access tools are the query and reporting tools, which can be deployed cost-effectively for a large number of users. These tools have extensive formatting capabilities, but cannot answer complex questions that require drill-down capabilities. Other types of tools are included in the following list:

- Spreadsheets such as Excel
- Tools that can access multidimensional databases
- DSS tools that can perform multidimensional analysis against relational databases
- Data-mining tools
- Statistical-analysis tools, which can perform complex statistical analyses
- Artificial intelligence and advanced analysis tools

183 What is the challenge that front-end tools are required to address?

The challenge is to create a reporting environment where the needs of all users can be met. This requires balancing the needs of the vast majority of nontechnical users, whose requests fall within limited parameters, with the requirements of some users who demand performance and flexibility. Such a reporting environment must be scalable and secure within a controlled environment; its deployment must meet the varying demands of business users and avoid straining IT resources. If the reporting tools are underutilized by the users and do not meet their expected potential—which can be caused by a number of reasons—the result will be a data warehouse that is considered to be of limited success or a failure.

184 What are the requirements of data access tools?

Data access products must meet several basic requirements:

- Ability to meet the diverse needs of users
- Wide variety of functions
- Ease of use
- Flexibility
- Ability to easily create ad hoc reports
- Scalability
- Performance
- Low implementation cost
- Fast deployment
- Web access and access options (desktop, smartphone, etc.)
- Support for different output types
- Formatting capabilities
- Export capabilities
- Adaptability to changing business needs
- Database connectivity
- Scheduling flexibility
- Compatibility

- Distribution options
- Ease of administration
- Security
- Integration with other tools (such as MS Office)
- Vendor reputation and support

Many of these variables will be considered during any evaluation; the most important factor, however, is the ability of the tool to meet the needs of the users.

185 What is a dashboard?

A dashboard is a business intelligence software application. It is a data visualization tool that consolidates and presents, on a single screen, different items that can be used for reporting, analysis, monitoring, and control. The consolidation of information enables the user to quickly, at a glance, observe what is happening, because the dashboard highlights any abnormalities. The items that can be displayed within a dashboard are key performance indicators (KPIs), metrics, static and dynamic reports, tables, graphs, charts, dials, links, scorecards, and the like. The data can be presented in real time or there could be a time lag.

An organization can have multiple dashboards. A dashboard can be organized into tabs for specific roles, departments, and so forth, in order that focused and relevant information can be presented. For example, a dashboard can comprise the following tabs: Executive, Operations, Sales, Revenue, Bookings, CFO, Regional, Historical, and Trends. Each tab will contain relevant information pertaining only to the tab heading.

186 What are dashboard challenges?

A dashboard must answer a business question or resolve a business problem. It must display all the required information in a single screen layout that can be quickly assimilated, clearly and without distraction. It needs to be exceptionally well-organized, concise, and clear; must emphasize summaries and exceptions; and should contain customized information. A user viewing a dashboard should be able to quickly perform analyses without scrolling, drilling, or clicking off the initial screen.

A dashboard should be designed so that it retrieves only the data that is required for analysis or it can potentially degrade the performance. Dashboards need to be simple and to avoid clutter. They should use different levels of complexity for different types of users. A balance should be maintained between drill-downs and guided navigation. Charts should be used to present different data views. Visuals should be carefully selected, as all visuals do not provide the same effect.

187 Which KPIs should be displayed on a dashboard?

The KPIs displayed on a dashboard should be actionable and "drill-able" in order to enable access to additional details and to conduct further analysis. KPIs should be benchmarked with industry standards, if possible or cost effective. The metrics should be compared with baselines, expectations, or averages. The number of metrics displayed should be limited. Too many KPIs can be confusing because users typically find it difficult to simultaneously focus on more than three to seven KPIs. Within a dashboard, the total number of KPIs should be limited to 20.

188 What is a scorecard?

A scorecard is a tool that is linked to an organization's business strategy and performance goals. It displays KPIs, together with their associated performance targets. For example, a regional revenue scorecard, monitored by a CFO, will contain the revenue for each region as well as its target revenue. If a gauge is being used for presentation, the scorecard's dial needle will indicate, at a glance, which regions are scoring well, and those that are underperforming and need attention. Using drill-down, the underperforming areas can be investigated and the underlying data analyzed to determine the reason for the abnormal result.

In contrast to a dashboard, which provides the status as of a given moment, a scorecard indicates the progress, or lack thereof, toward specific goals. A scorecard can be displayed on a dashboard.

CHAPTER 21

TOOL SELECTION AND DATA MINING

189 How should a front-end tool be selected?

A data access front-end tool should be selected with the end-users in mind and must be able to satisfy their needs and requirements. The tool should interface with end-users, who are often nontechnical, in business terms rather than cryptic technical jargon. It should be easy to use, flexible, allow ad hoc querying by unsophisticated users, and should not require heavy usage of IT resources for the creation of reports and queries.

The tool needs to be sold to both business executives and end-users. They should be involved as early as possible in the selection process, which should be presented as a joint venture between the implementers and users. Input should be elicited from all types of users, as well as IT, before selecting the front-end tool. If all impacted users and IT are involved, a high tool-adoption rate will be ensured.

To make the tool selection exercise a success, a few sound principles should be followed:

- Follow an acceptable methodology for selection
- Specify the selection criteria
- Document the user requirements
- Specify IT requirements
- Consider and evaluate at least three vendors
- Request product demos
- Involve users as well as IT in the testing

190 Is it better to build or buy a front-end access tool?

The decision to buy or build depends on many factors and requirements, including the number and types of reports, desired analytics capability, architecture and platform, and distribution features. It is usually better to buy a third-party tool for a number of reasons. The vendor can regularly provide the latest functionality upgrades, support for the tool and for multiple platforms, multiple report distribution options, training, implementation flexibility, and consulting. In-house development can be less cost effective over the long term and will require the continuous availability of highly skilled developers who can maintain and enhance the tool.

191 What can be the consequences of selecting the wrong tool?

The selection of an inappropriate tool can create many issues during implementation, as well as ongoing operations. Many tools, although adequate in some environments, are incompatible with other tools used at a particular implementation. Therefore, all tools and components should be evaluated and selected carefully. The choice of the front-end tool, in particular, can have far-reaching implications. The data warehouse will either fail or not achieve any measurable success if it is not easy to use or does not provide the functionality required by its users. Hence, the data access tool, which must be intuitive and user-friendly, must be selected after thorough evaluation.

192 What is an efficient way of leveraging report-development resources?

The availability of powerful front-end access tools has been an important driver for the popularity of data warehousing. However, although power users have successfully mined data warehouses, end-users have not used the reporting tools to their full potential. Most of them limit their usage to executing predefined starter queries and reports provided to them. In a dynamic business environment, changes occur all the time. Therefore, when such users are unable to modify even simple reports, they are forced to seek IT help. However, creating or modifying simple reports is not the optimal use of highly skilled IT resources. Hence, a large pool of power users should be created so that the maximum benefit is gained from the data warehouse.

193 Who are the leading front-end access tool vendors?

At this time, there are many vendors who each provide a complete suite of data warehousing products and services. There are several leading vendors of front-end access tools:

- SAP (Business Objects and Crystal Reports)
- IBM (Cognos and SPSS)
- SAS
- Oracle (OBIEE)
- Microsoft
- MicroStrategy
- Information Builders
- Others include LogiXML, Actuate®, and Clarity®

The following are open-source vendors:

- Jaspersoft
- Pentaho
- Eclipse BIRT®
- GNU Enterprise

194 How should a data-access tool vendor be selected?

An inappropriate tool or component can create many problems and, in the worst case, even cause a data warehouse to fail. Therefore, a data access vendor should be selected with extreme care after evaluating the pros and cons of the following two approaches:

- Best of breed
  - Best product for each category or component, including the front-end tool, chosen and then integrated
- Turnkey project
  - All the major components for creating the data warehouse—from ETL through end-user access—provided

An approach that works quite well in the long term, in most cases, is to have a flexible architecture that will meet current needs as well as future requirements. Such an approach supports the implementation of best-of-breed tools over time and allows the easy replacement of individual components.

195 What is data mining?

Data mining is a technique that analyzes large volumes of data for determining patterns and relationships, using advanced statistical analysis and modeling techniques. Conceptually, the objective is to generate a hypothesis and correlate factors that can be used to analyze and improve the business. For example, a credit card company might use data mining to determine potential defaulters.

196 Who uses data mining?

The heaviest users of data mining, a technique that is still in its infancy, are retailers and telecommunication companies. It is widely used in the banking, insurance, healthcare, and transportation industries. Retailers mine data to determine which products are bought together, which path the customer follows through the store, and which sales-floor layouts are most effective. Data mining can unveil strange but useful associations. For example, a retailer discovered that almost half of the customers who bought diapers on Friday evenings also bought beer—an association that led the retailer to display the two products next to each other.

197 What is data mining based on?

Data mining is based on a number of algorithms including neural networks, induction, association, fuzzy logic, and visualization. The probability of finding patterns is increased as the number of algorithms used is increased.

198 Where can data mining be applied?

Data mining applications can be implemented in a wide range of scenarios:

- Identifying buying patterns
- Predicting responses to advertising

- Uncovering credit card usage patterns and fraud
- Identifying the behavior of risky or fraudulent customers
- Retaining customers
- Identifying potential new customers
- Analyzing product failure
- Identifying new business opportunities

199 What are the basic differences between OLAP and data mining?

OLAP answers specific questions; data mining aims to discover patterns in the data. For example, OLAP can provide the average transaction amount for credit cards, stolen versus non-stolen. On the other hand, data mining can uncover buying patterns associated with the fraudulent use of credit cards or can identify churners—those who are more likely to switch phone carriers.

CHAPTER 22

FEATURES OF FRONT-END TOOLS

200 What are the basic features of front-end tools?

All the front-end tools, of which there are many, support a basic feature—the ability to generate reports interactively. The interaction is based on a selection of variables (facts, dimensions, and filters), in various combinations, that enable the business to be analyzed from different perspectives. The basic features of these tools include drilling (down and across), filtering, positioning/hiding totals, swapping, pivoting, exporting, converting currencies, displaying results graphically, manipulating and/or formatting results, charting, and sorting.

Some of the commonly desired features, which are essential for analysis and for professional presentations, are described in the following sections.

201 What is slicing and dicing?

The slicing and dicing technique, which refers to the rearrangement of data so that it can be viewed from different perspectives (such as by period and cost center), is an essential and very widely used feature. This technique enables the data returned by a query to be displayed in different ways, by manipulating the initial results that are displayed. For example, the initial query results can present the total sales for each region. Using the slice and dice technique, the displayed results can be manipulated so that the sales for each state are displayed. Further slicing and dicing can lead to the display of sales by state, by product line, and by store.

202 What is drill-down?

The drill-down technique enables navigation from the summary results to the underlying detailed data. For example, a store manager can execute a report that, initially, displays the total store sales. Using drill-down, the sales for each product group in the store can be presented. If more comprehensive analysis is required, the manager can perform additional drill-down so that the sales for each product item in the store can be displayed.

203 What is drill-across?

The drill-across technique is similar to drill-down with the difference being that the drilling is done horizontally, rather than vertically. For example, after the annual sales results have been queried and displayed, the drill-across feature can be used to display the sales for each month.

204 What is a condition?

Conditions are formulated with the objective of retrieving and analyzing data based on restrictions that narrow query results. For example, a ranking list condition can be applied so that the query returns the results for the top ten customers (in terms of sales dollars, number of orders, etc.) or the three best performing brands. Similarly, by specifying a numeric value limit, the results can be restricted to numbers that fall above (or below) a certain threshold value or within a range. Several conditions can be defined within a single query. Conditions can be modified, activated, or deactivated, as required.

205 What is an exception?

An exception defines a numeric value deviation from a predetermined threshold value in order to highlight abnormal or critical results. Any results that fall outside a set of predetermined threshold values and intervals can be displayed in different colors or fonts so that the variances are highlighted, thus providing an opportunity to take appropriate action. Exceptions, which can be displayed as highlighted cells, can be prioritized (such as good or bad) and can be color coded.

206 What is summarization?

This feature enables analysis to be performed against summarized data, rather than detailed data. Senior management and executives prefer to run queries against summarized data sets, rather than against detailed transaction data, because it provides a higher-level view that is more useful to them.

207 What is involved in swapping axes?

This function enables the switching of rows with columns in a report. For example, if the regions are displayed in the rows and the months are displayed in the columns, executing the swap function will cause the regions to be displayed in the columns and the months to be displayed in the rows. The data returned by the query will remain the same, though the display will be different—but more meaningful to the analyst.

208 What is a jump function?

A review of the results returned by a query might indicate that further in-depth analysis is required, which could require the execution of another report or navigation to the source data. The jump function enables another report to be directly executed and accessed from the currently displayed report.

209 What are commonly used navigation techniques?

When a query is executed, it provides an initial view of the results, which can be modified using various navigation techniques:

- Filtering a characteristic by characteristic values or hierarchy nodes
- Drilling down by characteristic and then changing the drill-down status
- Filtering a characteristic and drilling down using a different characteristic

- Keeping a filter value for retaining a characteristic that has been selected as a characteristic value or hierarchy node
- Hiding and displaying key figures
- Distributing characteristics and key figures along the query's row and column axes
- Changing the sequence of characteristics and key figures on an axis
- Expanding a hierarchy
- Switching active hierarchies on and off
- Reverting to the original report display after some navigation steps have been performed within the report

210 Which presentation functions are desirable?

The ability to display results that are esthetically appealing and have a professional appearance are common reporting requirements. Some of the basic requirements include the ability to format reports by manipulating the font, size, colors, patterns, styles, alignment, graphics, and so forth. The importance of these features depends on the report consumer. For reports that are distributed to external customers, such as the company's annual report, the presentation features are very important.

211 What are other desired front-end tool functions?

A number of other features are desired in front-end tools. One of the most popular is the ability to sort and export to other applications such as MS Excel, where the results can be processed further or subjected to additional formatting. There are other features as well:

- Scheduling
- Distributing
- Filtering
- Scaling factors

- Binning (custom grouping)
- Displaying characteristics' properties
- Personalizing through favorites
- Querying with preselected variables values
- Providing alerts
- Creating dashboards

212 What is the Context Menu?

The Context Menu is a useful tool that enables navigation in many ways and provides many additional functions. When it is available, it can typically be accessed by clicking the left or right mouse button, which pops up a menu of functions from which an appropriate selection can be made. The functions that are displayed for selection when the Context Menu is activated depend on the cell context.

213 What are the typical Context Menu features?

The Context Menu contains many functions and features, ranging from basic to very advanced:

- Basic navigation techniques such as back, forward, back to start (for undoing navigation steps that have been executed), and go to
- Retained filter value (for displaying only the data for a characteristic value, whereas the characteristic value itself is removed from the drill-down)
- Retained filter value on axis (for displaying the data for a characteristic value, if the characteristic value itself is to be displayed in the drill-down)
- Selection of filter value for filtering by values
- Drill-across or drill-down
- Ability to remove drill-down

- Filter and drill-down capabilities according to a characteristic set at a certain value (filter) and a simultaneous drill-down using another characteristic on the same axis (row or column)
- Capability to swap query axes; if key figures are in columns and characteristics in rows, swapping causes characteristics to be displayed in columns and key figures in rows
- Ability to swap a characteristic/structure with another characteristic/structure
- Hierarchy expansion (expanding or collapsing hierarchy nodes)
- Hierarchy activation or deactivation
- Sort function for ascending or descending order
- Sort function for characteristic values or attributes for a drill-down characteristic
- Ability to cumulate individual cells in an area
- Currency translation
- Ability to apply simple bookmarks as well as bookmarks with data
- Ability to export to Excel and CSV files
- Ability to change different settings for the characteristic or key figure
- Ability to change query properties

CHAPTER 23

DATA MARTS

214 Which data warehouse limitations became data mart drivers?

Data warehouses have provided many benefits that organizations have leveraged to their competitive advantage. Enterprises have been forced to seek alternative solutions for their information needs, however, because of some of the following data warehouse limitations:

- Lag between need and implementation—it used to take a very long time, sometimes years, from the time a data warehouse was requested till the time it was actually rolled out to the users.
- Huge size and scope of data warehouse projects encompassing the entire organization—such projects were very expensive, costing millions. They also spanned a very lengthy period and, in some cases, took years to implement.
- For enterprise implementations, which spanned disparate computer systems and numerous departments, complexity and integration proved to be overwhelming for most IT departments.
- Conflicting requirements, priorities, and the schedules of different departments and business units derailed many projects.
- Politics ruled.
- Cost overruns and delays were common.

All these problems became the drivers that have led to the development and widespread growth of data marts in the past couple of decades.

215 What are data mart characteristics?

The following characteristics define data marts:

- Do not have to be based on the enterprise data model
- Are typically limited to one or a few subject areas (such as sales and finance)
- Each contain only a small part of an organization's data; enterprise can have many
- Can be implemented as a small project and within months
- Are easy to design, build, and test; are less expensive to implement and maintain
- Have far fewer users than a data warehouse
- Can have one or multiple sources—a data warehouse, another data mart, or an OLTP database
- Have databases that are far smaller—typically only a few gigabytes
- Require simpler hardware and supporting technical infrastructure
- Can be implemented by staff with less experience and fewer technical skills
- Are typically built by different project teams without a common design, process, tools, hardware, or software
- Can be built independently, in a staggered manner, as needs evolve
- Can make possible future integration difficult to achieve because of independent construction

216 What are the characteristic differences between data marts and data warehouses?

The following is a list of important data mart characteristics and how they compare with those of a conventional data warehouse:

- Data marts aim to meet a department's needs, whereas a data warehouse is designed for the enterprise.

- IT staff with limited or no data warehousing skills can implement a data mart, whereas highly skilled IT professionals are required to build an EDW.
- A data warehouse spans the entire organization and covers most subjects, whereas a data mart covers only one or a few subject areas.
- A data warehouse is designed using an enterprise data model and is constructed by a large central specialized professional team; data marts are constructed by different, small, project teams.
- In contrast to data warehouses, data marts need not be based on the enterprise data model structure.
- Data warehouses are integrated; data marts are not.
- Data marts can be linked together, if required, but that task can be challenging.
- Although a data warehouse is typically unique, an organization can have many data marts, built by different teams, without a common design.
- The result of independent construction is that data mart integration, if required at a later stage, is difficult to achieve, whereas data warehouses are integrated from the beginning.
- Data marts are easy to design and build, which makes them less expensive to implement and maintain; designing data warehouses is very complex and time consuming.
- A data mart, although it can store gigabytes of data, usually contains only a small segment of an organization's data; most of the enterprise data is stored in an EDW.
- A data warehouse needs to be planned and implemented as a huge project, which is not the case with data marts.
- Uniformity exists within a data warehouse project; however, it is missing when data marts sprout because various implementation groups might use different processes, tools, hardware, and software.

217 What are the advantages of data marts?

Data marts are characterized by many advantages and benefits, which are listed below:

- Simpler
- Less risky
- More focused
- Can be implemented in months instead of years
- Can be implemented in phases
- Scalable
- Flexible
- Can obtain easy and fast approval
- Not dependent on IT budget
- More affordable; budget can be a few hundred thousand dollars instead of millions (required for an EDW)
- Use low-cost hardware and software
- Avoid political conflicts associated with data warehouse projects
- Require fewer and less sophisticated resources
- Can be linked to other data marts or data warehouses
- Can improve performance by storing the data closer to the users

218 What are the disadvantages of data marts?

Although many benefits are associated with implementing data marts, there are also some disadvantages:

- Data marts cannot support a key requirement of an EDW—the ability to analyze enterprise-wide data across business units.

- Their development can be uncoordinated, which creates a hurdle when data marts are used as the building blocks for creating an EDW.
- Their design is not as thorough as that of a data warehouse and, consequently, consideration for an ultimate upgrade to an EDW is inadequate or lacking.
- Every data mart has its own narrow view.
- The age-old problem with multiple legacy systems can also afflict data marts—a query might yield different answers depending on which system was accessed, when it was accessed, and how the query was structured and executed.
- Redundant and inconsistent data can make "one version of the truth" a casualty.
- Growth of data marts creates more redundant and inconsistent data, which has a cost associated with it and poses problems during upgrades.
- Design flaws and the number of data extracts can restrict scalability; data marts might be unable to support massive data volumes associated with data warehouses.
- Clandestine development and operations might be encouraged.
- More work is required in reconciling terms, definitions, data, and business rules when data is migrated to an EDW.
- They are designed and built by less experienced personnel, which can affect the quality of the product.
- Multiple databases are required to be maintained, which can be inefficient and could require greater breadth of technical skills.
- The extraction process can be different for each data mart.
- Activities such as extraction and processing are not centralized; activities can be duplicated and additional staff can be required for maintenance and support.

- Tools, software, hardware, and processes can be different for each data mart.
- Knowledge gained by one data mart group may not be shared with other groups.
- They can be expensive in the long run.

However, despite all these potential issues, when a cost/benefit analysis is performed, the benefits to the business far outweigh the negatives, which is the reason data marts are so popular and widely implemented.

219 How are data marts loaded?

There are two primary ways in which data is usually loaded into a data mart:

- Data is fed from an EDW to the data mart(s); any changes to the EDW are propagated to all associated data marts receiving its feeds.
- Data is fed to the data mart(s) by direct extract(s) from the source system(s).

220 Which platforms and tools can be used by data marts?

Data warehouses and data marts have been implemented on many platforms including Unix and Windows. Implementation of such projects involves many technologies, tools, hardware, and software, which range from the very simple to the very sophisticated. Although some vendors dominate in specific areas, such as ETL or databases, and some have offerings across the range of products required for implementing a data mart or data warehouse, no vendor dominates in all areas. The data mart vendors, with some exceptions, are the same as the data warehouse vendors.

CHAPTER 24

IMPLEMENTATION APPROACHES

221 What are the common data warehouse/data mart implementation approaches?

There are two widely used approaches for building data marts:

- Top-down
  - Build an EDW and then construct dependent data marts, which are its highly summarized subsets.
- Bottom-up
  - Build independent data marts, whose foundation is the enterprise data model, which can then be used to construct an EDW.

The other approaches used to build data warehouses include the hybrid, the federated, and the hub-and-spoke method.

222 What is the top-down approach?

In this approach recommended by Bill Inmon (Figure 6), the data warehouse is planned as the corporate central repository. In this architecture, a normalized data model is used, with the data being stored at the lowest level of detail or granularity. After the enterprise data warehouse is developed, dependent data marts are constructed and are fed by the data warehouse. Whereas a data warehouse is difficult to implement, data marts are relatively simple to construct because they are developed for specific departments or business processes.

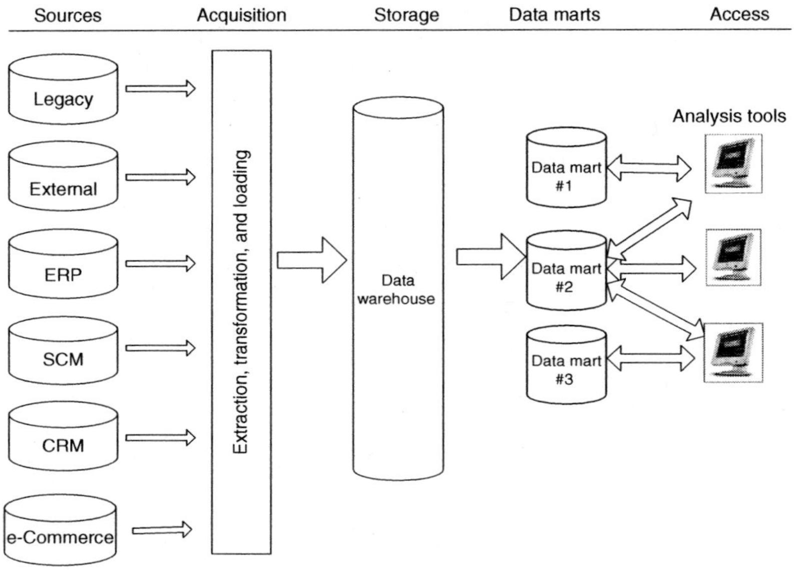

FIGURE 6 Top-down architecture.

223 What are the characteristics of the top-down approach?

The characteristics defining the top-down approach are as follows:

- Is methodology-based; addresses important aspects such as modeling and implementation
- Provides an enterprise-wide view of the organization
- Has a well-planned architecture
- Is implemented based on well-documented requirements

- Avoids integration issues that characterize data warehouses derived from data marts
- Permits better control and quality, because the EDW drives the construction of dependent data marts
- Unable to respond to business needs in time, long delivery cycle, high cost, project delays, cost overruns, and other issues associated with large projects

224 What are the drawbacks of the top-down approach?

The primary disadvantage of the top-down approach is that it requires a major project for implementation, because of the massive scope of work that is involved. Consequently, it has a high cost and risk associated with it. The up-front cost for implementing a data warehouse using the top-down methodology is significant and the time involved, from the start of project to the time that end-users experience initial benefits, can be significant. Also, during implementation, this methodology can be inflexible and unresponsive to changing requirements.

225 What is the bottom-up approach?

In the bottom-up approach, independent data marts, whose foundations are the enterprise data model, are built first. These data marts, usually designed for specific business processes or departments, can be combined subsequently to construct the enterprise data warehouse as shown in Figure 7. Their integration is accomplished through what is known as a "data warehouse bus architecture," which involves joining the data marts together by conforming the dimensions. When the same dimension tables are used by different dimensional schemas, the tables are known as conforming dimensions. They enable drill-down from one schema to another and join measures from different star schemas. Conformed dimensions can be used across any business area, because they allow queries to be executed across star schemas. They can be used to analyze facts from two or more data marts.

This approach is recommended by Ralph Kimball, the well-known data warehouse expert.

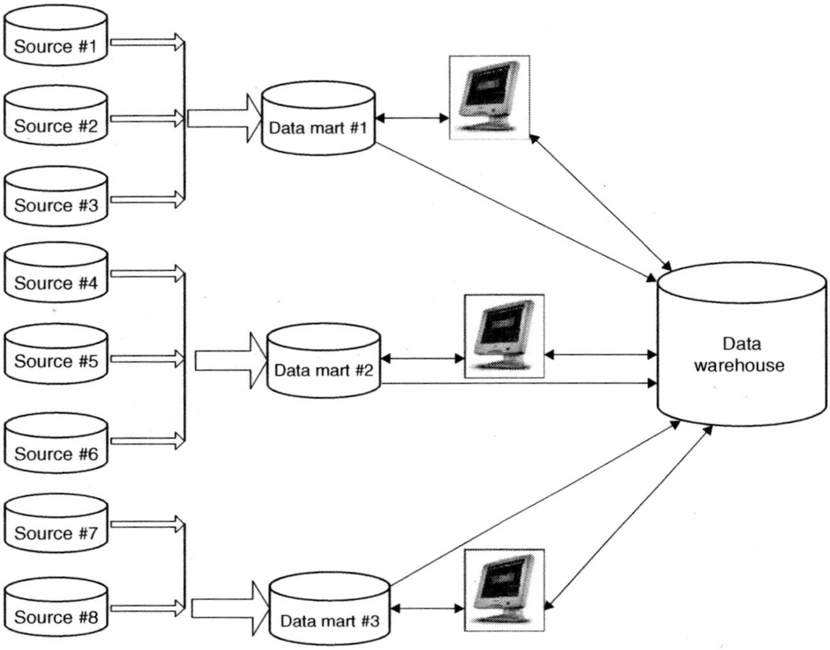

FIGURE 7 Bottom-up architecture.

226 What are the characteristics of the bottom-up approach?

The characteristics defining the bottom-up approach are as follows:

- This approach can meet some enterprise-wide needs, because data marts can be combined seamlessly for reporting and analysis.
- Seamless and transparent integration, although possible, is technologically challenging and performance can be poor, especially if many data marts need to be integrated.
- The bottom-up approach can lead to the sprouting of data marts and data redundancy.
- Lack of adherence to standards can cause major issues, especially integration problems, when an EDW is constructed from multiple data marts.

- Fast implementation provides less time for analysis.
- Implementation is not difficult.
- Implementation can be accomplished in phases.
- Implementation risk is lower.

Other benefits and characteristics, as well as disadvantages, of this approach are listed in Chapter 23, "Data Marts."

227 What is the hybrid approach?

Both the top-down and bottom-up approaches have their advantages and disadvantages, leading to the hybrid approach, which tries to find a middle ground. It provides faster implementation, just as the bottom-up approach. However, it also leverages the data and design consistency, as well as the integration benefit, of the top-down approach.

In the hybrid approach, the requirements are defined at the enterprise level, followed by definition of the data warehouse architecture. Next, the data content is standardized. Finally, a number of data marts are implemented in sequence. The enterprise data model is implemented in an iterative manner, with the heavy duty infrastructure being implemented at a later stage, only when the need for enterprise reports becomes a requirement.

228 What is the federated approach?

The federated approach tries to leverage existing deployed systems by integrating them when required because of changing business needs or conditions, such as mergers and acquisitions, cross-functional requirements, organizational changes, and other events. These systems can include decision support structures, OLTP systems, data warehouses, data marts, and applications. The benefit is that the existing infrastructure does not need to be discarded and the organization can be more responsive to changing business needs.

229 What is the independent approach?

In this approach, data marts are built randomly, without any enterprise planning or consideration of a common data model. This approach can lead to anarchy over a period of time.

230 Which approach should be used?

All the approaches are characterized by various pros and cons. Each approach meets the needs of many different types of organizations and users. The decision to select a particular approach is influenced by many factors, such as the relative importance of the various selection variables for the organization considering an implementation.

The selection variables can be diverse and can include project objectives, budget, timeline, availability of funding and resources, complexity of the environment, new or upgraded implementation, scalability, state of existing infrastructure, and so forth. For example, if the objective is to have something up and running quickly, or the budget is limited, the obvious choice is the data mart bottom-up approach. However, if strategic concerns and long-term considerations are driving the requirements, and the company is prepared to spend millions for a well-designed system, the top-down approach for implementing an EDW will be the appropriate choice.

CHAPTER 25

INMON VERSUS KIMBALL

231 What is the Inmon approach?

Bill Inmon is a data warehousing pioneer who provided the widely accepted definition of a data warehouse, which is based on four characteristics—subject-oriented, integrated, nonvolatile, and time-variant. His basic approach is to plan for an EDW using the top-down approach. In this architecture, the data warehouse can be used to feed any associated data marts. The Inmon methodology, as well as the Kimball methodology, has been widely used for implementing data warehouses. There are several other characteristics that define the Inmon approach:

- "Big-bang" implementation
- Use of well-known database development methodologies and tools
- Data warehouse—part of the Corporate Information Factory (CIF), the broader corporate information environment
- More dependent on IT professionals, which provides better technical solutions
- Secondary role of business users

232 What is the Kimball approach?

Ralph Kimball is one of the pioneers of data warehousing. He is credited with dimensional modeling or the Kimball methodology, which is one of the most widely used for implementing data warehouses. According to this approach, a data warehouse is the combination of various data marts, all of which are stored in the dimensional model. The Kimball approach includes other defining characteristics as well:

- Conventional database development methodology not followed
- Data mart built for each process
- Multiple data marts to meet all the needs and to create a data warehouse
- Data marts connected via data bus

233 What are the similarities between the Kimball and Inmon approaches?

The following are the defining similarities between the two approaches:

- Time-stamped data
  - Kimball – Date dimension
  - Inmon – Time element
- ETL process
  - Inmon – Data loaded into the data warehouse
  - Kimball – Data loaded into the data marts
- Business requirements gathered first
- Users can query by time period

234 What are the differences between the Kimball and Inmon approaches?

The following are the defining differences between the two approaches:

- Complexity
  - Inmon – Complex
  - Kimball – Simple

- Analysis
  - Inmon – Extensive analysis performed
  - Kimball – Limited analysis performed
- Primary focus
  - Inmon – IT professionals because of nature of methodology, architecture, and development approach (spiral); leads to IT ownership
  - Kimball – Business users because of simpler development methodology
- Development methodologies
  - Inmon – Top-down
  - Kimball – Bottom-up
- Implementation
  - Inmon – Big-bang
  - Kimball – Incremental
- Data-modeling approach
  - Inmon – Subject-oriented or data-driven
  - Kimball – Process-oriented; users can participate actively
- Tools
  - Inmon – ERDs
  - Kimball – Dimensional modeling
- Data warehouse architecture
  - Inmon – EDW serves the entire enterprise and feeds departmental data marts/databases
  - Kimball – Single-process data marts connected via a data bus and conformed dimensions

235 Which characteristics favor Kimball?

Each of the defining characteristics can favor either Inmon or Kimball, depending on the requirements and needs of the organization considering the data warehouse/data mart implementation. Therefore, although the answer is enterprise/project specific, some generalizations can be made regarding the characteristics that favor Kimball.

The Kimball methodology is favored when the needs are tactical rather than strategic, implementation is urgently required, budget and scope are limited, resources are limited and lack top-notch technical skills, integration across the enterprise is not required, and focus is on the analysis of business metrics.

236 Which characteristics favor Inmon?

The Inmon methodology is favored when the needs are strategic rather than tactical, implementation can be performed over a very long period, budget is very large and scope is enterprise-wide, resource constraints are limited and top-notch technical professionals are available, integration across the enterprise is required, and focus is on nonmetric data as well as data that can be used for varied needs across the enterprise.

237 Which approach is better?

Both the Kimball and Inmon approaches have been widely implemented over the past couple of decades. They have met the varied and specific needs of enterprises as well as departments. The approach to be selected should meet the users' needs and must not be based on a dogmatic belief. Depending on the specific requirements, either approach could be appropriate. For example, if the time frame is short and budget is limited, Kimball's approach is the obvious way to go. On the other hand, if the requirement is an EDW, covering the needs of the enterprise spread over many regions, and the organization is flush with cash, then Inmon's approach should be selected.

238 How should the approach be selected?

The following are some items that should be included in the list of variables to be considered when selecting the approach:

- Scope (EDW or departmental)
- Implementation schedule
- Budget
- Environment/infrastructure
- Technology requirements
- Availability of technical expertise
- Culture
- Operating cost
- Data availability and quality
- Expected growth

CHAPTER 26

MULTIDIMENSIONALITY

239 What are the analysis limitations in data warehouses?

The introduction of data warehousing technology shifted the focus from collecting to analyzing data. The tools available for analyzing data warehouse data, however, were limited in the types of analysis that they could perform. For example, they could not perform complex analysis along multiple business dimensions or at different levels of aggregation. Neither could they present multidimensional views or results in different formats. Consequently, many users felt an acute need for faster, flexible, and more innovative techniques that would help them answer complex questions and support decision making. The solution developed to overcome the data warehouse limitations and fulfill the needs of its users, was multidimensional analysis, which is also known as OLAP.

240 What are the limitations of two-dimensional traditional databases?

Traditional relational databases, as well as spreadsheets, are based on a two-dimensional model of rows and columns. Such a model allows a user to view data in two dimensions, such as sales by region. Data warehouse users rarely want to access data through only one dimension (or column). For example, a wireless carrier analyst will not limit the analysis to determining just the number of new customers. Such an analyst will typically add another dimension, such as phone manufacturer, to determine the number of new customers by phone manufacturer (Apple, Blackberry, Nokia, etc.). For even more in-depth analysis, the analyst may add another dimension—phone model (iPhone, Curve, Bold, etc.). This will enable the "new customers by manufacturer by model" analysis to be performed. This scenario can continue to become more complex as more dimensions are added.

The two-dimensional model cannot support the requirement to relate multiple dimensions in order to understand the relationship between different dimensions. However, most data warehouse queries are multidimensional, which use multiple criteria against multiple columns. Therefore, data warehouse users will be severely limited if they are restricted to a model that supports only two dimensions.

241 What is required to conduct analysis via more than two dimensions?

In a relational database, analysis of multiple dimensions will require the setup of a series of tables, such as customer, region, distribution channels, and the like. The next step will require the appropriate tables to be joined and, subsequently, accessed through complex Structured Query Language (SQL) code, which would enable the desired analysis to be performed.

242 What are the drawbacks of joins?

The need for joins, which are not difficult for programmers to implement, forces users to consider the data structure. Multidimensional analysis overcomes this limitation by enabling data to be accessed through multiple dimensions or columns (criteria), which are presented in business terms and, hence, can be selected easily without knowing the underlying data structure. For example, a user can analyze sales by product by region over time by picking the appropriate dimensions, which are displayed in the data warehouse presentation layer by their business names (sales, product, region, and time).

243 What is the dimensional model?

The dimensional model overcomes the limitations of relational databases, which are organized in a two-dimensional format. The dimensional model is based on a structure organized by dimensions, such as sales or region, and is represented by a multidimensional array or cube. This model, in which data is organized according to a business user's perspective, provides an intuitive way of organizing and selecting data for querying and analysis.

244 What are the benefits of the dimensional model?

A multidimensional model offers several benefits:

- Enables powerful analytical processing
- Permits data to be easily analyzed across any dimension and level of aggregation
- Is representative of the company's business model
- Organizes data according to a business user's perspective
- Overcomes the limitations of two-dimensional relational databases
- Provides a view that is business oriented rather than technical; users can concentrate on the business instead of the tool
- Is flexible
- Enables slicing and dicing, which provides the ability to analyze data using different scenarios and dimensions

245 What is a dimension?

Wikipedia defines a dimension as "a data element that categorizes each item in a data set into non-overlapping regions" (*http://en.wikipedia.org/wiki/Dimension_(data_warehouse)*). A dimension can also be viewed as a structure, often composed of hierarchies, that is used to analyze business measures or metrics, which are also known as "facts." A dimension, examples of which are customer, region, and time, enables data warehouse data to be easily sliced and diced.

246 What are the characteristics of a dimension?

A dimension represents an attribute such as product, region, sales channel, or time. All data warehouses have one common dimension—time. A spreadsheet is the simplest example of a two-dimensional model. The spreadsheet row and column names are the "dimensions" and the numeric data in it are the "facts." A time dimension can include all months, quarters, and years, whereas a geography dimension can include all countries, regions, and cities. A dimension acts as an index for identifying values in a multidimensional array. If the number of dimensions used is increased, the level of detail that can be queried becomes greater.

247 What is a slowly changing dimension?

A dimension that changes over time is called a slowly changing dimension. For example, the price of a product might change, a region could be renamed, or the address of a customer might change. Such changes are implemented in different ways. For example, the old record can be replaced with a new record, which causes the history to be lost. The two other methods used to capture attribute changes include creating an additional table record with a new value and creating a new field in the dimension table (where the old dimension value is stored).

248 How can a three-dimensional model be represented graphically?

Figure 8 represents a three-dimensional model with state, product, and time dimensions.

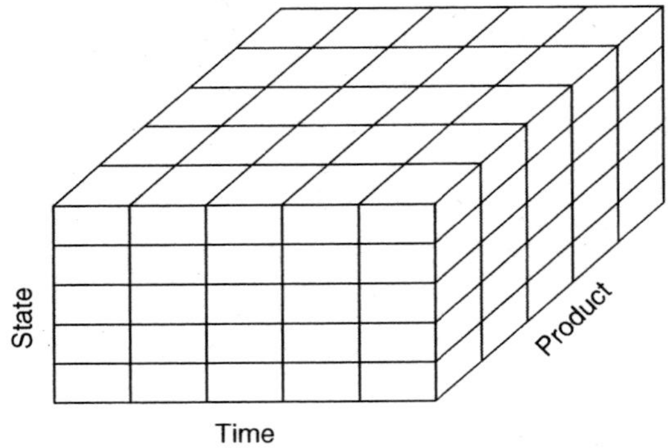

FIGURE 8 Three-dimensional model.

249 How can multiple-dimension views be represented graphically?

Figures 9 and 10 demonstrate how multiple dimensions can be used to represent different views of the same data.

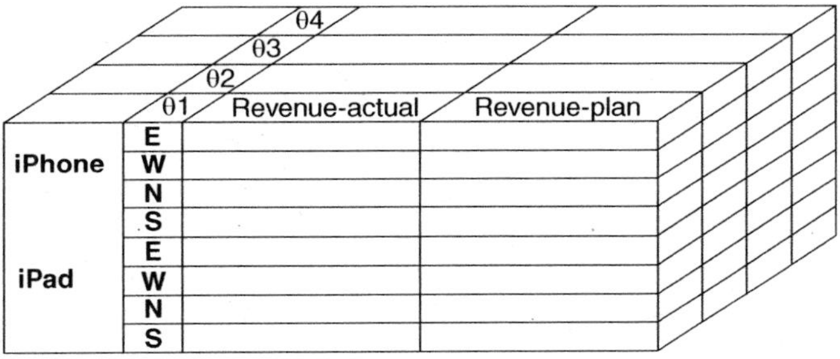

FIGURE 9 Multiple-dimension views—product.

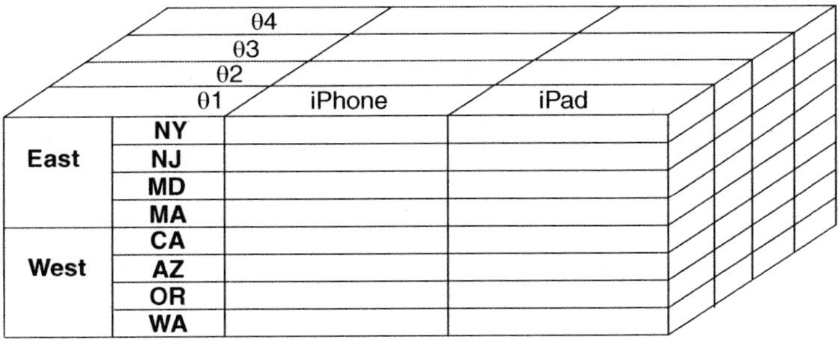

FIGURE 10 Multiple-dimension views—region.

250 What is a cell?

If a single member is selected from all dimensions, then a single cell is defined. A three-dimensional model is represented by a cubic structure in which each dimension forms the side of a cube.

251 How can a single cell be represented in a dimensional model?

Figure 11 displays how a single cell can be represented, in a dimensional model, after drilling down to the lowest level.

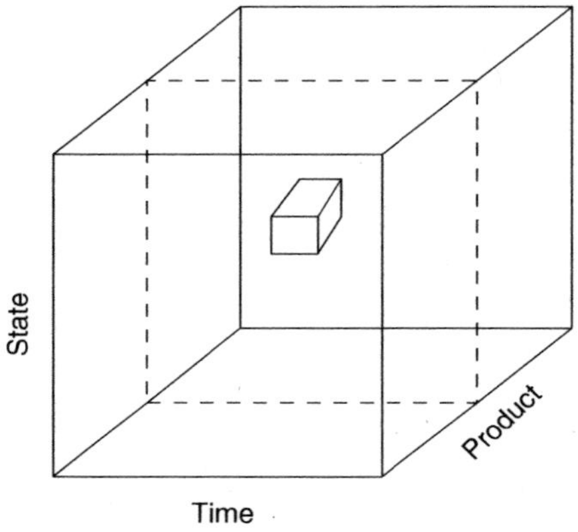

FIGURE 11 Drill-down to a cell.

252 How can slicing and dicing be performed along different dimensions?

Figure 12 demonstrates how data can be sliced and diced along different dimensions.

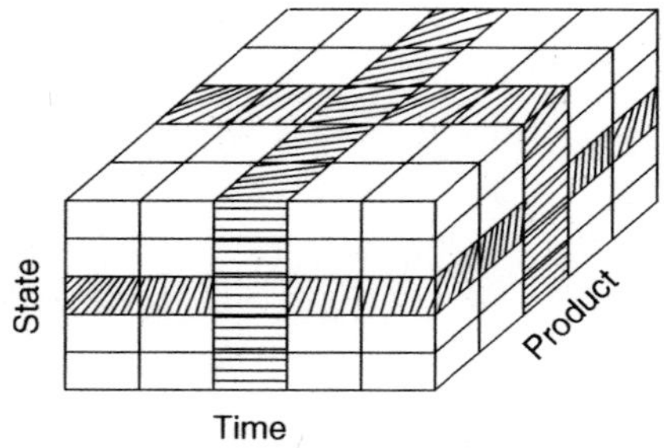

FIGURE 12 Slicing and dicing along multiple dimensions.

CHAPTER 27

FACTS AND DIMENSIONS

253 What is a fact?

A fact is a business measure or metric that is used to measure business performance such as sales, revenue, units sold, and costs. Facts are contained in the fact table in a star schema. They are the values, in the array in a dimensional model, which change over time.

254 What are the different types of facts?

There are three types of facts:

- Additive
  - The most common – a measurement that can be added across all dimensions in a fact table; examples include revenue, profit, sales, and cost
- Semi-additive
  - Can be added for some dimensions only, such as headcount
- Non-additive
  - Cannot be summed for any dimension

255 What are the characteristics of a fact table?

Dimensional queries are based on the data in the fact tables. The fact tables contain two types of fields that store the following data:

- Foreign key – connects each fact to the appropriate value in each dimension
- Individual facts – cost and quantity

The following list outlines the defining characteristics of a fact table:

- Is the primary table that contains numeric data—measurements such as price, cost, profit, and salary
- Holds the "real" quantitative data—the data being queried; typically holds atomic and aggregate data such as the number of cars sold
- Has fact table row corresponding to a measurement
- Contains all the attributes to be measured
- Takes measurement at intersection of all the dimensions—month, product, and region
- Consists of multiple columns and a large number of rows (can be millions)
- Has fact attributes that contain measurable numeric values (which are normally additive)
- Restricts numerical measures to fact tables
- Has facts that can be operated on (summed, averaged, aggregated, etc.)

256 What is fact table granularity?

Granularity refers to the lowest level of detail that is stored in a data warehouse fact table. For example, the lowest level of data can be maintained at the yearly, quarterly, monthly, weekly, daily, or hourly level. Depending on which level of detail is maintained, the analysis that can be performed will vary significantly. For more in-depth reporting capability, low granularity is preferred.

Granularity is a variable that influences the design considerably. Before designing a fact table, the desired granularity has to be determined, which is primarily driven by the requirements and business needs. These also need to be balanced with the infrastructure and technology limitations.

257 What are the characteristics of a dimension table?

Dimensions, which are stored in dimension tables, permit categorization of transactions. For example, the customer dimension can be used to analyze procurement by location, frequency, buyer, vendor, and so forth.

A dimension table has the following additional characteristics:

- Reflects business dimensions such as product, region, and distribution channel
- Contains a primary key that connects it to the fact table
- Has dimensional attributes that provide links between the fact table and its associated dimension tables
- Contains descriptive data reflecting business dimensions; dimensional attributes provide description of each row in the fact table
- Groups descriptive attributes about the facts
- Contains many attribute fields; each field describes individual characteristics of the dimension; for example, attributes of product dimension can be description, size, color, weight, and type
- Used to guide the selection of rows from the fact table
- Has smaller tables with fewer numbers of rows
- Has denormalized tables; does not increase storage significantly; dimension tables are very small compared with the fact table

258 Which dimensions should be included?

The dimensions to be included in the data warehouse are driven by the reporting and analytical requirements. Every dimension that is required and specified in the requirements documents, for creating every report, query, scorecard, and dashboard, must be available in the data warehouse. However, if future needs are also considered, then it makes sense to include additional dimensions, especially if they can be designed and loaded without any significant effort or cost.

259 How can analysis be performed through a single dimension?

Tables 3–5 show how multidimensional analysis can be used to analyze revenues by region, subregion, and quarter, using multiple dimensions, for a multinational corporation (MNC). The company analyzes its revenues according to its two regions:

- America
- Rest of the World

In Table 3, the analysis is performed via a single dimension—region. It displays the consolidated revenue, $300 million, as well as the individual revenues for each region, "America" and "Rest of the World," which are $100 million and $200, respectively.

TABLE 3 Analysis via Single Dimension

Region	**Revenue (in millions)**
America	$100
Rest of the World	$200
Total	**$300**

In Table 3, there is only one fact (revenue) that is related to a single dimension (region). The only dimension in this case (region) is used for aggregating its associated fact (revenue).

260 How can analysis be performed through two dimensions?

If the MNC desires to analyze the performance for each subregion, it can drill down so that the revenues for each region and subregion, as shown in Table 4, are displayed.

TABLE 4 Analysis via Two Dimensions

Region	**Subregion**	**Revenue (in millions)**	
America	North	25	
	South	15	
	East	23	
	West	37	
		100	Subtotal
Rest of the World	Asia	70	
	Europe	80	
	South America	30	
	Middle East & Africa	20	
		200	Subtotal
		300	Total

Table 4 relates one fact (revenue) to two dimensions—region and subregion. It shows the revenues associated with each of the eight combinations of region and subregion dimensions.

261 How can analysis be performed through three dimensions?

If the MNC desires to analyze even more comprehensively, it can use a third dimension (time), as shown in Table 5, which relates one fact (revenue) to three dimensions (region, subregion, and quarter). Table 5 displays the aggregated revenue (fact) for each combination of region, subregion, and time.

TABLE 5 Analysis via Three Dimensions

Region	**Sub-Region**	**Quarter**	**Revenue**	**Totals**	
America	North	Q1	6		
		Q2	7		
		Q3	5		
		Q4	7	25	Sub-Total
	South	Q1	3		
		Q2	3		

(*Continued*)

TABLE 5 (*Continued*) Analysis via Three Dimensions

Region	Sub-Region	Quarter	Revenue	Totals	
		Q3	4		
		Q4	5	15	Sub-Total
	East	Q1	6		
		Q2	4		
		Q3	8		
		Q4	5	23	Sub-Total
	West	Q1	9		
		Q2	9		
		Q3	8		
		Q4	11	37	Sub-Total
				100	**Total for America**
Rest of the World	Asia	Q1	15		
		Q2	19		
		Q3	16		
		Q4	20	70	Sub-Total
	Europe	Q1	20		
		Q2	24		
		Q3	16		
		Q4	20	80	Sub-Total
	South America	Q1	7		
		Q2	6		
		Q3	8		
		Q4	9	30	Sub-Total
	Middle East & Africa	Q1	4		
		Q2	5		
		Q3	6		
		Q4	5	20	Sub-Total
				200	**Total for Rest of the World**

CHAPTER 28

OLAP

262 What is OLAP?

Online analytical processing (OLAP) is a business intelligence tool that addresses the need to perform multidimensional analysis. It is based on an analytical technique that combines data access tools with an analytical database engine. In contrast to the rows and columns structure of relational databases, OLAP uses a multidimensional view of data (such as sales by brand, season, and store).

Query outputs are presented in a matrix or pivot, where the columns and rows are the dimensions. The values in the matrix are obtained from the measures, which are derived from the fact table records. The dimensions are derived from the dimension tables.

OLAP is used in a wide variety of applications, including budgeting and forecasting, sales, business process management, financial reporting, and marketing.

263 What are OLAP characteristics?

The 12 guidelines or rules proposed by Dr. Codd, inventor of the relational model for database management, for an OLAP system are used to determine if it is conforming to those principles and to compare OLAP tools and products. These rules include multidimensionality, accessibility, transparency, consistent reporting performance, flexible reporting, unlimited dimensions and aggregation levels, and multiuser support.

264 What are the characteristics of OLAP data?

An OLAP system has a number of basic defining characteristics:

- Multidimensional
- Analytical
- Easy-to-use interface
- Fast
- Flexible
- Shared and secure
- Summarized data
- Far less data storage than a data warehouse
- Client/server architecture support

265 What are benefits of OLAP?

OLAP is a technology that provides many benefits. It enables users to access data quickly, efficiently, interactively, and in innovative ways without first having to understand the data structure or technical details. The data, which is presented in dimensions as business users view it, can be queried and analyzed using different views. Compared with data warehouses that are based on relational database technology, OLAP systems have an additional feature—the ability to perform "what if" analysis, a powerful tool that can simulate the effect of decisions.

The following list outlines important benefits that are associated with OLAP:

- Supports multidimensional analysis
- Enables valuable insight to executives, managers, and analysts
- Identifies key trends and factors driving businesses
- Increases innovation and productivity of individuals and organizations
- Provides ability to drill down/across, perform complex calculations, as well as trend analysis
- Provides ability to manipulate data with many interrelationships

- Provides ability to interact with the data
- Insulates users from SQL language and the relational model
- Improves query performance
- Enables large data volumes to be analyzed rapidly
- Provides high scalability
- Supports a wide range of tools
- Can present data in many formats
- Automates maintenance of indexes and summaries
- Decreases demand for reports from IT
- Used in a wide range of applications such as forecasting, profitability analysis, customer analysis, budgeting, and marketing analysis

266 What are OLAP limitations?

All the OLAP models and tools have certain limitations in terms of functionality, compatibility, scalability, performance, and cost. For example, while relational OLAP (ROLAP) systems store data in standard relational databases, their schema can be quite complex. A proprietary data structure, despite being stored in a relational database, can make a product incompatible with another product's schema. Additionally, ROLAP systems make a trade-off in terms of significantly reduced performance and functionality, as well as the cost of implementation, but outperform in the ability to handle larger amounts of data compared with multidimensional OLAP (MOLAP) systems.

267 How does OLAP impact the data warehouse?

The implementation of an OLAP system within a data warehouse system impacts the performance with regard to the technique used to process queries. Some of the data warehouse queries, which can be very complex and can overtax performance, can be offloaded to the OLAP system. Consequently, when the load is shifted to the OLAP system, the data warehouse performance will improve. Additionally, the query previously being executed in the data warehouse will run considerably faster in the OLAP system, which is specifically designed for that purpose.

268 What are the desired OLAP features?

Many characteristics and features are desired in an OLAP system:

- Consistent and fast query performance
- Ability to perform operations against single or multiple dimensions (aggregated, summarized, and derived data)
- Support for large data sets and unlimited dimensions and aggregation levels
- Scalability—large data volumes as well as the number of concurrent users
- User perspective—data should be transparent to users
- Ease of use
- Flexible reporting
- Intuitive data manipulation
- Seamless presentation of historical, projected, and derived data
- Time intelligence that supports analysis, such as year-to-date and period-over-period
- Powerful calculation capabilities
- Support for statistical and analytical functions
- Support for more than simple aggregation or roll-ups, such as share calculations (% of total) and allocations
- Ability to read data while updates are occurring
- Reasonable implementation cost
- Cost-effective maintenance
- Secure and concurrent access to data
- Integration with desktop tools
- Easy and fast deployment

CHAPTER 29

OLAP MODELS

269 What are the OLAP models?

OLAP can be implemented in various architectures:

- MOLAP – Multidimensional OLAP
- ROLAP – Relational OLAP
- HOLAP – Hybrid OLAP
- DOLAP – Database OLAP (or Desktop OLAP)
- WOLAP – Web-based OLAP
- RTOLAP – Real-time OLAP

270 What is MOLAP?

Multidimensional Online Analytical Processing (MOLAP) is the classic OLAP technology, which stores data in multidimensional format. The storage is in proprietary format, not in a relational database, and the data is presummarized to improve query performance. The technique is characterized by multidimensional indexing, optimized storage, and caching.

271 What are the advantages of MOLAP?

MOLAP queries executed against multidimensional array data are very fast and efficient. Besides superior performance, MOLAP cubes are ideal for slicing and dicing. MOLAP includes additional advantages as listed below:

- Better handling of aggregate data
- Calculations are performed when the cubes are created

- Less data, because of compression, compared with relational databases
- Superior performance of complex calculations
- Natural indexing because of array models

272 What are the disadvantages of MOLAP?

There are some disadvantages of MOLAP as well:

- Can handle only a limited amount of data
- Provides slower data loading for large volumes
- Has limitations in the data types it can store
- Provides a proprietary solution, which is more expensive
- Has limitations in querying dimensions with high cardinality
- Has a problem working with models having more than ten dimensions (for some MOLAP tools)
- Includes data redundancy

273 What is ROLAP?

Relational Online Analytical Processing (ROLAP) is an OLAP technology that competes with MOLAP. It stores data in a relational database format but provides a multidimensional view of the data to the users. ROLAP does not require the data to be precomputed before it is stored. When a user makes a request, ROLAP obtains the data from a relational database and then generates an appropriate SQL query. ROLAP can also summarize data, based on various combinations of data, through aggregations and summary tables.

274 What are the advantages of ROLAP?

The following are the key advantages associated with ROLAP:

- Stores data in a relational database
- Can handle very large data volumes

- Supports aggregation
- Can access data via SQL statements
- Has higher scalability
- Can handle large numbers of dimensions
- Provides faster indexing
- Provides faster data loading
- Provides more flexibility, in modeling, than a pure dimensional model
- Can leverage relational database functionalities
- Can leverage relational database authorization control features
- Performs better than MOLAP when dealing with nonaggregatable metrics

275 What are the disadvantages of ROLAP?

The following are the key disadvantages of ROLAP:

- Slower performance than MOLAP
- ROLAP report is basically an SQL query, which limits its functionality
- Not suitable for calculation-heavy queries
- Shortcomings due to skipping the creation of aggregate tables
- Custom ETL code required to load aggregate tables

276 What is hybrid OLAP?

Hybrid OLAP (HOLAP) is another OLAP technology variation, which combines the features of MOLAP and ROLAP. Some of the data is stored in MOLAP format (multidimensional database—MDDB), while some of the data is stored in a format that ROLAP can use (relational database). Therefore, this enables the leveraging of MOLAP's superior processing as well as ROLAP's ability to work with larger data volumes. Depending on the type of processing that is required, either one can be used. When summary-type information is needed, HOLAP leverages cube technology for faster performance. When detail information is required, however, HOLAP can "drill through" from the cube into the underlying relational data.

HOLAP has good scalability, can perform fast preprocessing, stores aggregates using MOLAP, stores detailed data using ROLAP, and reduces storage requirements; it is complex to implement and maintain.

277 What is database OLAP?

Database online analytical processing, DOLAP, is another OLAP variation that uses multidimensional cubes. It is also known as Desktop OLAP. DOLAP cubes, which are created dynamically by the DOLAP tool, are downloaded to the user's desktop, where query processing takes place. This OLAP model is aimed at the low end-user, whose limited analytical needs can be met by much smaller cubes.

CHAPTER 30

MULTIDIMENSIONAL DATABASE

278 What is a multidimensional database?

A multidimensional database is a proprietary database that stores data in an array format, in cubes, rather than the normal tables used by relational databases. This structure, which is a variation of the relational model—the most widely used database type, organizes and stores data according to predefined dimensions. Multidimensional data structures can be visualized as cubes of data. They are defined by the following characteristics:

- A cell is a single point in a cube.
- Each data item is located, and accessed, based on the intersection of the dimensions defining it.
- Each side of a cube is a dimension that represents an attribute or category (such as product, region, channel, or time period).
- Each cell contains aggregated data that relates the elements along each dimension.
- Using the dimension numbers that define them, data items can be easily located and accessed.
- An intermediate server can be used to store precalculations.

In this architecture, business users can view data via multiple dimensions, which they can relate to and understand. The result is that they can easily navigate through various dimensions and data levels and, consequently, are able to analyze the data easily and quickly. For databases using OLAP applications, the structure of choice is the multidimensional structure.

279 What is the OLAP database server?

The multidimensional data model is used by databases designed for OLAP applications. An OLAP server shown in Figure 13, which is an OLAP system's back end, is designed to specifically work with multidimensional data structures to enable fast, efficient, and ad hoc data retrieval. The server can store the data in an MDDB or a relational database. It has the option of either staging the data or populating the structures in real time on the fly. The database requirements are not large, because it can import the data from a relational database.

The key component of an OLAP server is its calculation engine. It is optimized for ad hoc query processing and data manipulation. The server can pull data in real time from other databases and, when needed, perform any required manipulations.

OLAP servers use a variety of operating systems, including Unix, Windows, Linux, as well as z/OS. Many vendors provide OLAP servers including Oracle, MicroStrategy, IBM, Microsoft, MISConsulting SA, Pentaho, Jedox® AG, SAP, and the SAS Institute.

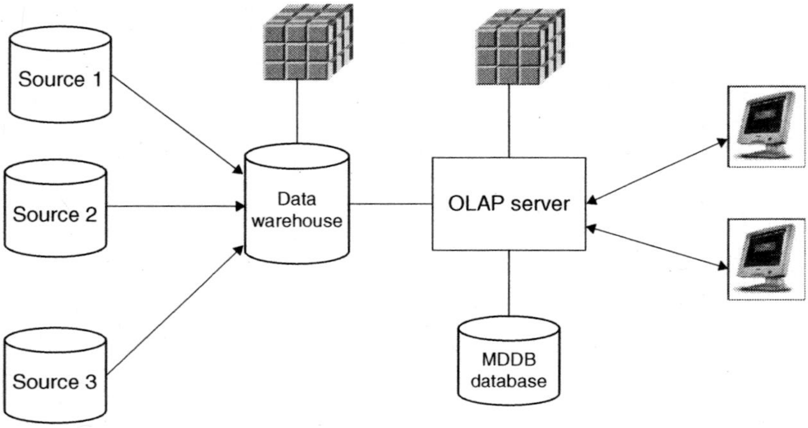

FIGURE 13 OLAP Server.

280 What are the key characteristics of an OLAP server?

The following list outlines the desired key characteristics of an OLAP server:

- Support capability for various OLAP types, such as MOLAP and ROLAP
- Fast and efficient query processing
- Reliable database
- Capability for real-time aggregation and calculation
- Real-time modeling, so that cubes can be created on the fly
- Ability to handle large data volumes
- Write-back capability
- Supports industry standards
- Multithread query engine
- Parallel storage
- Ability to compress infrequently used data
- Memory caching of data that is queried frequently
- Memory cache for faster access
- Summarized data optimization
- Centralized metadata
- GUIs for building and maintaining cubes
- Java support
- Easy server monitoring and maintenance
- Ability to extend application via APIs and standard serial interfaces

281 What factors need to be considered for evaluating OLAP products?

The following is a list of variables that can influence the selection of the OLAP tool and vendor:

- Multidimensional functionality
- Size of the cube(s)
- Performance
- Flexibility
- Platform for deployment
- Installed cost
- Integration with the database
- Integration with existing tools, including third-party tools
- Ability to leverage parallelism provided by database and hardware
- Types of calculations supported – summarization, precalculation, derivation, and aggregation
- Formulae
- Ability to drill down, drill across, roll up, and pivot (along one or more dimensions)
- Ability to perform various time functions such as year/year, year-to-date, periods (current or historical), moving averages, etc.
- Vendor history and reputation
- Implementation plan (in-house or consulting)
- Security
- Metadata support
- Maintenance cost
- Ease of administration

CHAPTER 31

OLAP: COMPARISONS, TOOLS, AND VENDORS

282 How does OLAP compare with a typical data warehouse?

Data warehouses store data in a denormalized relational format, which is informational. On the other hand, OLAP has a multidimensional structure, which provides analytical capabilities. It is relatively quite versatile and goes far beyond data access. Its capabilities include drill-down, slice and dice, as well as complex calculations and modeling. The size of the OLAP server is far smaller than the data warehouse, which stores huge volumes of very detailed data.

283 How does OLAP compare with OLTP?

OLTP systems are primarily used to run an organization's business operations. OLTP functions are performed by business applications that routinely capture business transactions in various business processes such as order management, human resources, procurement, production, and so forth. In contrast, the objective of OLAP systems is to analyze the data, especially for long-term strategic decision making, even though it is now extensively used for day-to-day operations. Examples of OLAP applications include trend analysis, sales analytics, revenue and costs, and customer profiling.

TABLE 6 OLTP and OLAP Comparison

OLTP	OLAP
Contains a snapshot of the current data (6–24 months)	Requires a history of transactions spread over many years (5–20+ years)
Updated continuously	Static data
Can have errors or missing data	Validated and complete data
Processes millions of transactions per day	Updated periodically through batch processing—usually once per day
Current data	Current and historical data
Large amount of data	Considerably less data
Limited reporting can be performed	Very flexible and powerful reporting
Uses entity-relationship diagram	Uses multidimensional model

284 How does MOLAP compare with ROLAP?

Both OLAP types have advantages and disadvantages associated with them. Compared with each other, MOLAP and ROLAP are superior in some categories, the importance of which depends on the particular implementation. In MOLAP, data is stored in a special OLAP database server, after being extracted from various sources, in preaggregated cubic format—in multidimensional arrays, rather than tables—using proprietary technology. This data remains static until an extract from the source system(s) adds more data to it. In contrast to this approach, ROLAP does not require an intermediate server because it can work directly against the relational database. Consequently, it can perform analysis on the fly. ROLAP uses SQL for data retrieval.

285 Which characteristics define MOLAP and ROLAP differences?

The leading features and differences of the two leading types of OLAP are listed below:

- MOLAP highlights
    - Data stored in relational database tables

- Proprietary MDDBs used to store summary data
- Data warehouse used for accessing detailed data; MDDB used to access summary data
- Data volumes limited
- Faster access
- Easy analysis across numerous dimensions
- Powerful and flexible drill-down capabilities
- Superior performance due to specialized indexing and storage optimization
- Less storage required because of leveraging compression technology
- Precomputation and data storage required in the cube
- Performance satisfactory with 10 or fewer dimensions; ROLAP can scale considerably higher
- Performance degradation at 10 dimensions or about 50 gigabytes of data; ROLAP can scale considerably higher.
- Database explosion possible, caused by excessive storage being used; this can be caused by the large number of dimensions, precalculated results, etc.
- More suitable for financial applications where the data can be broken down and is smaller
- Extensive complex analytical functions available

- ROLAP highlights
  - Data stored in relational database tables
  - Lightly summarized and detailed data
  - Very large data volume
  - More scalable for larger volumes
  - Ad hoc queries and aggregate data performed much faster—even with a constantly changing and much larger amount of data

- Inferior query performance compared with MOLAP
- Limited complex analytical functions
- Not restricted by the number of dimensions, type or number of users, database size, or complexity of the analysis
- Drilling possible but not easy or flexible
- Can leverage parallel scalable relational databases
- Significant degradation of performance when large volume preprocessing is skipped because of issues in implementing it efficiently
- More reliant on the database for performing calculations, which limits the functionality that can be used
- More suitable for applications in which a huge amount of data needs to be analyzed, such as marketing and point-of-sale

286 What is the convergence trend?

There is a trend toward convergence between MOLAP and ROLAP. MOLAP vendors recognize the need to drill down to the lowest level of detailed data, which their tools are currently unable to do, because of the limited data volumes/levels that are loaded into the MOLAP cubes. On the other hand, ROLAP vendors recognize that faster queries are desired and, hence, they are incorporating MOLAP features into their own products.

287 Which are popular OLAP tools?

There has been a lot of consolidation in this industry and some of the leading tools, such as Business Objects and Cognos, have been acquired. Hence, lists of vendors and tools are expected to continue changing because of consolidations, mergers, and acquisitions. The following is a list of well-known OLAP tools:

- BusinessObjects™
- Cognos™

- Hyperion
- OBIEE
- Microsoft Analysis Services
- MicroStrategy OLAP Services
- Mondrian™ OLAP Server
- Palo™ OLAP Server
- SAS OLAP Server

288 Who are the OLAP vendors?

At this time, OLAP tools are available from a large number of vendors:

- SAP (BusinessObjects)
- IBM (Cognos)
- Oracle (Hyperion and OBIEE)
- Microsoft (Microsoft Analysis Services)
- MicroStrategy (MicroStrategy OLAP Services)
- Pentaho (Mondrian)
- Jedox AG (Palo OLAP Server)
- SAS Institute (SAS OLAP Server)
- Information Builders (WebFOCUS)

The largest vendors in the OLAP market are Microsoft, Oracle, SAP, IBM, and MicroStrategy. There are many smaller upstart vendors who are introducing products, with some supporting SaaS, including Birst™, Oco, and GoodData®.

289 Who are the MOLAP vendors?

The following vendors provide MOLAP products:

- Oracle
- IBM

- SAP
- Microsoft
- MicroStrategy
- SAS
- Jedox AG
- Information Builders

290 Who are the ROLAP vendors?

The following vendors provide ROLAP products:

- Oracle
- IBM
- SAP
- Microsoft
- MicroStrategy
- SAS
- Pentaho

291 Who are the HOLAP vendors?

The following vendors provide HOLAP products:

- Oracle
- SAP
- Microsoft
- MicroStrategy
- SAS

CHAPTER 32

PLANNING FOR THE DATA WAREHOUSE INITIATIVE

292 What are the three phases of business intelligence strategy?

The business intelligence strategy can be categorized into three distinct phases:

- Strategy
  - High-level business intelligence needs are identified.
- Planning
  - Planning for the data warehouse project starts taking shape.
- Requirements
  - Requirements to be met by the data warehouse are identified and documented.

293 What are the business intelligence implementation critical success factors?

There are many variables that determine whether a business intelligence implementation will be a success or a failure. However, a few critical success factors have been identified; these can influence the ultimate success or failure of a data warehouse project:

- Clear objectives
- Good planning

- Strong sponsorship
- Implementation using a proven methodology
- Experienced project management
- Requirements that match user needs
- User involvement during planning and implementation
- Performance
- Scalable and reliable architecture/framework

294 What are success indicators?

The success of an implementation is usually indicated by a few valuable indicators. These include "one version of the truth" information becomes easily available, number of users increases rapidly, more time is spent by the average user mining the data warehouse, and the variety and sophistication of queries starts to increase.

295 What should be included in the basic planning of a data warehouse?

A basic requirement is to determine the high-level strategic business and information requirements of the organization. They are the foundation upon which everything will be built. The roadmap should be laid out and the implementation plan should aim to achieve that goal in a single or multiple phases. Since an EDW will never provide the same level of benefits to various functional areas and types of user, the areas or processes to be implemented first should ideally be the ones that will help the organization achieve its strategic long-term goals. Therefore, the functional areas (i.e., subject areas) that can benefit the most from a data warehouse should be identified. Subsequently, the subject areas can be prioritized so that their implementation sequence can be determined.

296 Which key factors are considered when planning a data warehouse?

Any evaluation of a potential data warehouse has to be based on its value to the organization, which is related to the expectations that are associated with it. A key factor to be considered is the risk, whose assessment is essential for determining the potential viability of the proposed project. Another key factor to be considered and evaluated is the approach to be used for implementation, such as top-down or bottom-up. That decision will impact the cost, schedule, architecture, and complexity, among other considerations. Another key decision to be made is whether to use an out-of-the-box data warehouse/data mart from one of the leading vendors. Alternatives include customizing it or building a data warehouse by putting together components from different vendors.

297 How can lack of strategic planning create problems?

When data warehouse projects are implemented without proper planning and consideration of their strategic importance to the organization, a number of problems arise. These issues are wide ranging and include failure to meet the requirements, inability to integrate and analyze the enterprise, rejection by intended beneficiaries, stakeholder issues, architecture problems, resource issues, integration issues, lack of ownership, incompatible or inadequate technology, and poor performance.

298 Why do implementation reason(s) need be identified?

Before embarking on a data warehouse project, it should be determined why the project is being undertaken, and management expectations should be understood. Is the need departmental or enterprise? Are operational, strategic, or tactical needs to be fulfilled by the data warehouse? How urgent are the strategic and operational reporting needs? Answers to these questions will clarify the project objectives and can influence important decisions regarding scope, architecture, methodology, and tools.

299 Why is sponsorship a prerequisite?

A data warehouse project has unique characteristics, which makes it a risky undertaking from the outset. The risk increases exponentially if sponsorship is lacking or weak. The project must be sponsored by a functional executive who is associated with the functional side—not IT—and who has a vested interest in the project.

Many data warehouse projects have failed due to lack of ownership, which can to lead to many problems such as lack of strategy, unclear objectives, weak project management, implementation issues, inadequate project funding, lack of appropriate resources, conflict between various groups and departments, poor coordination, undetermined scope control and other issues.

300 Which characteristics are desired in the sponsor?

The sponsor should be powerful, respected, capable of acting decisively, provide resources when required, force compromises, enforce decisions, communicate commitment to the project, keep a close eye on its progress, and step in without any delay when required.

The sponsor should have a personal stake in the success of the project and should have a project track record; he or she should be flexible, be unenamored by technology, and be user-oriented rather than technology-oriented. The sponsor should be able to encourage teamwork, to motivate, and to provide direction. It is a mistake to choose a sponsor who does not meet these basic characteristics.

301 What can happen if management is not on board?

Data warehouse projects demand a high level of commitment, and many have failed to meet expectations because of lack of management support. When support, which is required at various stages of the project, is lacking or denied, the project can face serious problems from lack of leadership and direction, funding issues, politics and conflict, failure to get adequate and appropriate resources, inability to resolve a wide range of issues requiring timely management intervention, and other challenges.

302 Why should business be the project driver?

A data warehouse is a business project rather than a technology project. Its objective should be to provide easily accessible data and information, rather than implementing state-of-the-art technology. It should be realized that technology will not solve all problems and, instead, should be used only as an enabler. However, some companies focus too much on technology because they are driven by the desire to be at the leading edge of hardware and software. Consequently, they focus on the technology—not the business and its requirements. This happens frequently when IT, whose focus is on technology rather than the business needs of the organization, drives the data warehouse project.

However, it should be realized that IT has a very important role to play, because it understands technology and how to implement it. Functional leaders do not always appreciate technical complexities and, hence, can become too demanding. Therefore, close cooperation between IT and business is required to ensure project success.

303 Why should a project's potential impact be evaluated?

The implementation of a data warehouse introduces new technologies, retires older ones, and has an impact equivalent to a reengineering project. The new architecture, which typically is a radical departure from the existing infrastructure, is the foundation upon which the new information architecture is based. It can impact company employees at all levels, ranging from senior executives to end-users, as well as IT staff. It suddenly empowers users and surprises entrenched managers, who find themselves in a position of less control. Attempt should be made to understand and appreciate the impact of implementing a data warehouse on both people and processes.

304 How can lack of, or flawed, evaluation cause problems?

A data warehouse system should not be implemented unless it is preceded by a thorough evaluation of the company's business, reporting, and analytical requirements, as well as existing systems—transaction and reporting. The potential impact of the new system, how it will integrate with or replace the organization's other applications, and how it will be accessed or delivered, should be carefully studied before a project implementation decision is made.

305 Is project justification necessary?

Data warehouse projects should be approached with the same thoroughness and preparation associated with any application development project. A data warehouse project should not be undertaken unless it has been justified through a cost/benefit analysis. A consulting partner or someone who is respected within the organization should perform the analysis. A well-justified project improves the probability of success and buy-in.

306 Why should a "one approach fits all" approach be avoided?

Even though some organizations may be similar, every organization is unique because of differences in company culture, hardware and software infrastructure, skill levels and technical expertise, budget constraints, business drivers, competition, objectives, management, and other characteristics. Also, business, systems, data sources, architecture, environment, components, project staff and skills, and constraints can be different. Therefore, every implementation is unique, defined by its own set of variables, even though there might exist many similarities with other projects. Hence, every proposed data warehouse project should be approached, evaluated, and implemented based on studying its specific requirements. If an approach is selected arbitrarily, without consideration of a particular organization and implementation, failure is assured.

307 Why should an overambitious approach be avoided?

When an organization implements its first data warehouse or data mart, it typically does not have experienced data warehouse professionals on its staff. Therefore, the risk of making serious mistakes is fairly high. However, despite lack of experience, many companies have chosen to implement enterprise-wide data warehouse projects without first gaining experience through a pilot or data mart project. Such an ambitious and risky approach, without experienced staff to guide it, often leads to cost overruns, delays, and project failures.

308 Why should analyzing the data and reporting environment be a prerequisite?

A data warehouse touches data scattered in various systems within an enterprise as well as, in many cases, external data. Before a data warehouse project is undertaken, the overall environment in which the business is operating and—if use of external data is planned—important external factors must be studied. The potential data sources, data silos, general state of data, and data initiatives must be identified and evaluated. The overall system and reporting architecture, current as well as planned, needs to be studied. Additionally, the legacy systems where the data is residing, methods and tools currently employed for reporting and analysis, and the types of users and their high-level requirements must be identified and analyzed before a project is undertaken.

309 Why should other data warehouse projects be studied?

A large enterprise could be operating multiple ERP systems, as well as other applications, such as decision support systems (DSS) and customer relationship management (CRM); these should be studied before an implementation is undertaken. Such systems, existing and planned, can impact the project scope, technical and business skills required, funding requirements, project ownership, implementation schedule, approach (top-down or bottom-up), methodology, and the like.

310 Why should readiness be determined?

Data warehouse projects are not easy to plan and implement. An organization considering an implementation must be prepared to adopt radical changes that can affect the architecture, techniques, tools, as well as operation and maintenance. For such a project to succeed, it must have the support of three key groups: management, those affected by the implementation, and those implementing it.

Therefore, before deciding to proceed with such a project, management's commitment and the organization's readiness for change must be determined. If management lacks commitment or it is determined that the organization is not ready for change, the project should be delayed until the conditions are more favorable.

CHAPTER 33

IMPLEMENTATION PREREQUISITES AND APPROACH

311 Which high-level tasks are performed during planning?

An unplanned project can mean potential disaster. Before a data warehouse implementation is started, it should be preceded by detailed planning, as described in the previous chapter. Such planning must define the scope and specifications, as well as specific responsibilities for the client, vendor, and consulting partner(s).

During planning, sometimes a number of tasks listed in the requirements and development phases are performed at a preliminary or high level, even though, logically, they should be performed during later phases. These include tasks such as database selection (relational/multidimensional), capacity planning, data refresh and update strategy, archiving strategy, among others, which can impact the implementation as well as routine operations and maintenance. In many projects, the implementation strategy, top-down or bottom-up, is also determined in the planning phase. However, the selected or preferred strategy can be changed, based on the results of the analysis phase.

312 Why must project objectives and goals be implementation prerequisites?

Before embarking on a data warehouse project, the project drivers and objective, as well as management expectations, should be determined. For example, the objective can be to provide departmental, operational, or enterprise reporting. However, the requirements for these three options are significantly different and, hence, their implementation cannot be expected to be the same.

Project objectives and goals should be clearly specified, which will ensure that there are no unrealistic expectations. Clearly defined objectives and requirements will influence important decisions such as scope, approach, architecture, methodology, and tools. Defining objectives will ensure that the project will not be risked because of ambiguities or misplaced expectations and requirements.

313 Why do guiding principles and business drivers need to be defined?

The guiding principles, which are a set of goals, should be defined to provide direction to the project team. These principles can be referred to throughout the project, especially when conflicts arise. The project business drivers also need to be defined at an early stage. They provide the means for quantitatively measuring success against metrics. Examples include revenue growth, customer retention rate, improvements in efficiency, and decrease in product failure or returns, among others.

314 What are the consequences of inadequate project funding?

Many projects have failed because they were started without the structure of a formal approved project and budget. In many cases, problems arose because projects did not have adequate budgets. In some cases, projects were initially funded for a specific period or phase with the expectation that additional funding would be forthcoming at a later stage. When such projects failed to obtain adequate or expected funding, they either failed or were scrapped.

315 When should scope be defined?

The scope must be finalized before project implementation begins. All the critical elements that can impact scope, such as the subject areas or cubes to be implemented and access method(s), must be identified and incorporated in the scope. If this is not done, scope creep—the bane of every IT project and one that frequently afflicts data warehouse projects—will derail the project.

316 How can scope be managed during the planning stage?

Scope must be controlled very tightly at every project stage. However, despite the best effort exerted by project management, scope does increase frequently because of the nature of data warehouse projects and the way requirements are finalized. The key is to minimize scope creep, if it cannot be eliminated completely. If scope is not carefully managed and controlled, risk will increase and the project will either exceed its budget or will fail to be completed on time.

Project scope can be managed by limiting the number of subjects to be implemented, number of departments to be included, number of data sources, and number or types of users; data warehouse size, analysis techniques, and customization can also be limited. Use of high-quality data sources, and selection of the platform to be implemented (existing or new) should also be considered carefully when attempting to manage scope.

317 Which implementation methodology should be used?

In the past couple of decades, as data warehouse technology has matured, the implementation approach has also changed. Instead of iterative methodologies, structured methodologies are now being widely used. The various methodologies reflect the experiences that implementers have gained over the years. The important point to note is that an implementation must not be carried out without a formal methodology—the roadmap for ensuring that a project is executed according to sound project principles. Some of the methodologies being favored at this time include Agile, ASAP, and Waterfall.

318 When and which implementation approach should be selected?

Data warehouses can be constructed using any of the implementation approaches described earlier. There are pros and cons associated with each approach. The approach to be selected depends on a number of variables, which vary from project to project. In general, if an EDW is required, funding can be easily obtained, and there is little pressure to deliver quickly, the top-down approach is recommended. However, if the need is urgent, funding is limited, and risk needs to be low, the bottom-up approach is recommended.

The implementation approach to be used, top-down or bottom-up, should be determined as soon as possible in the planning phase. The approach to be used is one of the most important decisions to be made because it impacts the architecture, risk level, budget, schedule, resources, sponsorship, scope, and project complexity.

319 What are the specific project prerequisites?

The following are prerequisites that should be met before starting a data warehouse project:

- Sponsorship available
- Cost justified
- Funding approved
- Source(s) and availability of required legacy and external data studied
- Size and type of data warehouse determined
- Existing and required infrastructure evaluated
- Location determined
- Operational challenges identified
- Resource limitations identified

320 Why should developer-centric projects be avoided?

A very widespread approach for implementing data warehouse projects is to use a few developers, who form the core of the implementation team. They are given a few months to come up with a system against which a few queries can be executed. Very little, if any, requirements-gathering is performed and, typically, no enterprise architecture or roadmap is developed. Most of these projects fail to meet their objectives because they rarely meet the real requirements and needs of the users.

321 What are the benefits of implementing a pilot project?

A pilot project has many advantages because it avoids the risks associated with a major project. After gaining valuable experience through the implementation of a small pilot project, an organization can leverage this experience and build a conventional data warehouse, with less risk. Other benefits include a smaller budget, a short implementation schedule, and scope limited to a small department or a single subject. If the pilot project fails, its impact will be limited to a small group, and the overall enterprise data warehouse initiative will not be derailed.

322 Why should implementation of best practices be pushed?

It is recommended that best practices and techniques should be used. Such a strategy will reduce risk and improve the odds of successfully executing a data warehouse implementation on time and within budget.

CHAPTER 34

COMMON MISTAKES AND RISKS

323 Why do barriers, challenges, and risks need to be identified?

Data warehouse projects are more complex and difficult to implement than conventional application development projects. In the planning stage, before such a project is started, the barriers, challenges, and risks associated with its implementation should be identified. Failure to understand them will significantly increase the risk and probability of failure. The challenges and risks that typically derail data warehouse projects are discussed in the following sections.

324 What are the common types of barriers?

Typically, the barriers are of two types. The first type is political and cultural and can be attributed to senior executives, functional department managers, data owners, IT, and business users. The second type of barrier is technical and is relatively easy to identify, evaluate, and manage. If these implementation barriers are identified at an early stage, the risk to the data warehouse project will be reduced.

The most common types of barriers include resistance from senior executives fearing loss of control, fallout resulting from lower-level staff empowerment, functional process owners not being on board, hidden political agendas, departments having their own decision support systems or working in silos, poor relationship with IT, and inadequate funding.

325 What can be the result of poor project planning and execution?

As with any major IT project, poor project planning and execution of a data warehouse project can lead to failure. All implementations should follow a well-proven methodology, such as Agile, and a well-defined project plan. Such a plan should be well managed and controlled. Many implementations have not met these basic requirements, however, and, consequently, have failed. In one implementation, which was executed without a formal project plan, over $800,000 was spent over a two-year period with no meaningful results.

326 What are the consequences of unclear project goals?

If the project goals are unclear or inconsistent, it could mean trouble for the project. In the worst cases, where the deliverables are not specified and controls are lacking, the project can run into many serious problems such as selection of the wrong approach, unrealistic schedule, poor architecture, faulty design, scope control, unrealistic requirements, disagreement over functionality, roles and responsibilities, implementation issues, integration, and other issues.

327 Why should a project not be implemented with an undefined scope?

When a data warehouse project is undertaken without clearly specified scope and requirements, the implementation is disorganized, schedules and scope changes are the norm, design changes occur frequently, development and testing are impacted negatively, developers and analysts become frustrated, resources are pulled in and out, sign-offs are difficult to obtain, and the end result is failure.

328 Why should a casual implementation approach be avoided?

Many data warehouse implementations are undertaken very casually on an ad hoc basis, without a detailed formal project plan. Stakeholders and impacted business owners are not engaged adequately. The reason for a casual approach is underestimation of the complexities and pitfalls associated with a data warehouse project. A data warehouse must never be implemented without the structure of a project plan that includes specific tasks, schedules, milestones, responsibilities, and deliverables, which need to be monitored constantly so that any deviations can be addressed immediately.

329 Why must risks be identified?

All data warehouse projects have risks associated with them, which should be identified by the project manager. If the risks are highlighted early on, the project risk will be reduced, because steps can be taken to eliminate or mitigate them. The risks can be numerous such as poor project management, inadequate budget, poor financial controls, unrealistic and flawed schedule, scope creep, critical or high resource turnover, lack of proper resources, poor communications, users unavailable for User Acceptance Testing (UAT), poor architecture, lack of management support, changing requirements, and changing priorities.

330 Is lack of project experience a risk?

The number and types of users involved with a data warehouse project can be quite varied. Stakeholders can be across divisions, geographies, business units, and departments. Personnel involved with the project can include consultants, business analysts, IT technical staff, line managers, senior management, SMEs, end-users, and ordinary workers. However, some of these project staff members have limited or no experience working in schedule-driven aggressive projects, data warehouse or non-data warehouse, which creates a challenging and risky environment.

331 What can be the impact of resource and schedule constraints?

The resources for a data warehouse project are made available for a specific period, after negotiations, by various departments and organizations. Any delay in using the resources can, in many cases, effectively mean that they will not be available when required. The complex and time-intensive nature of a data warehouse project, with hundreds of interdependent tasks, requires that schedule constraints must be carefully monitored if project success is to be ensured.

332 What are the potential financial risks?

A data warehouse project is always exposed to two risks: cost overrun and schedule slippage—both of which increase financial risk. They can have a negative impact on resources, can force scope reduction, can lead to competing demand for funds from other successful projects, can cause a window of opportunity to be missed, and can have other adverse effects. In the worst scenario, a delayed or over-budget project can be scrapped.

333 What can happen if expectations are not well managed?

In order to sell a data warehouse project, management expectations need to be raised. In some cases, however, such expectations are raised to unrealistically high levels, which can be an issue when they are not met. It is imperative that expectations be set very carefully—this can be a difficult task. If the expectations are not reasonably high, the project runs the risk of not being approved or its preferred resources might be allocated to a competing higher value project. If expectations are too high, and they are not subsequently met, the project will be considered a failure. Over the life of the project, expectations should be carefully managed, especially when issues arise and there are delays or unexpected forced scope changes.

334 What makes data warehouse projects political?

A number of factors make data warehouse projects very political. They can cause organizational and departmental boundaries to be crossed, open access to previously restricted data, empower those who had been denied access to valuable information, reengineer processes, and impact how work is performed by many groups. Sociotechnical factors, people, and politics, although they are relatively unimportant in conventional IT projects, are very important in data warehousing projects. In such projects, new rules exist and business users attain more power.

335 What is the impact of politics?

Politics is always a problem in data warehouse projects because many departments, entities, and IT, all with conflicting priorities and agendas, are involved. It can impact such a project at every step, including scope, requirements, selecting and prioritizing the subjects for implementation, data requirements and quality, project team selection, and access tool selection. Therefore, someone who is politically savvy and has superior project management skills should lead the project.

336 What is the reaction to loss of control?

Many executives fear loss of control and, therefore, are reluctant to let others encroach on their turf or provide needed buy-in. They create many different kinds of roadblocks, including superseding business needs, prioritizing from a point of self-interest rather than from the best interests of the enterprise, restricting access to data that others can use, and so forth. Frequently, there is conflict between functional users and IT, which views it as a technology project; IT does not favor the empowerment of business users and refuses to let the business drive the project.

337 What types of complexities can be expected?

A data warehouse project is technologically complex and difficult to execute and poses integration challenges, because of the greater number and sophistication of tools required to implement it. Many high-level skilled technical resources are required and it can involve many regions, hierarchy levels, departments, groups, and processes whose requirements can be in conflict because of different needs, pain points, priorities, and politics. Consequently, such factors can combine to create a complex, risky project that is under tremendous pressure to be delivered on time and within budget.

338 What are the integration challenges?

A data warehouse is fed data from multiple sources that can be residing on different platforms and systems, each using different technologies. The data from these sources is ultimately integrated inside the data warehouse after undergoing complex operations. The overall data warehouse process uses a variety of technologies, including databases, ETL tools, middleware, front-end reporting tools, and networks. Integrating all of them is a complex task and a challenge—from a technical as well as a business perspective.

339 Why can an integration challenge be overwhelming?

The integration complexity involved in a data warehouse project can be extremely challenging. Integration of diverse systems can be required across various processes, departments, and regions. The range of technical skills required for the integration effort are quite varied and can include data modeling, data cleansing, OLAP, SQL skills, programming, system administration, ETL, metadata management, interfaces, legacy systems, query development, dashboard development, and Web development. Many companies and implementation teams have been overwhelmed by the integration challenge and have failed to deliver a successful project.

340 How can deficient procedures create issues?

Procedural factors can play a part in the failure of data warehouse projects. These include poor or deficient implementation and deployment, undefined approval processes, lack of formal process for involving users, undefined process for upgrading pilot or small-scale data marts into an EDW, undefined and inadequate testing procedures, and absence of scope control mechanism, among others.

CHAPTER 35

PROJECT RESOURCES

341 Who needs to be on a project team?

Data warehouse project team members should be drawn from the various functional departments, representing the various processes being touched, as well as IT. The business functional experts should be among the most knowledgeable in their departments; they should be good decision makers with analytical skills, be highly motivated, and should have the ability to work in a team environment. The team members, who (with some exceptions), must be fully dedicated to the project; they must have the appropriate skills, knowledge, ability to work under pressure, and experience. They should preferably have a stake in the implementation.

342 What roles and skills are required for implementation?

The implementation of a data warehouse project requires many skills—technical and business. The right mix of business and technical resources should be provided to the project team. Some of them might be required on a part-time basis or only during specific project phases. The success of the project depends on the availability of the required resources. There are specific resources that are typically associated with such a project:

- Sponsor
  - Senior executive responsible for the overall project who, typically, chairs the Steering Committee
- Steering Committee
  - Responsible for ensuring that the project runs smoothly and is in sync with the corporate business and IT strategy; consists of functional staff drawn from various business areas as well as IT representative(s)

- Project manager
  - Responsible for project's strategic direction, monitors progress, and ensures that the budget and schedule are adhered to; manages the project and project team, provides progress reports, and is responsible for the success of the project
- Domain experts/SMEs
  - Provide functional expertise during requirements, design, and testing phases
- Business analysts
  - Functional and process experts who understand the business; represent the business, especially during the requirements and design phases, and bridge the gap between IT and the business
- End-users
  - Test and verify whether the data warehouse works as designed
- Technical experts
  - Perform various technical tasks involved in designing and constructing the data warehouse; they include architect, data modeler, and developers
- Quality assurance
  - Ensure that the data is validated and that the application, reports, queries, and dashboards work as designed
- Trainer
  - Creates the training materials and delivers training to the power users and end-users
- Consultants
  - Fill the gaps when internal resources are not available; can be very valuable, but their excessive use should be limited; it limits the retention of knowledge within the organization

343 Which technical roles are required for implementation?

There are many technical skill sets required to implement a data warehouse project. The technical skills span a variety of technologies, including legacy systems, ERP, data conversion and migration, operating systems, databases, networking, front-end access tools, Web technologies, and SQL. The technical roles that are required to implement these technologies in a data warehouse project typically include the following:

- IT support staff
  - Responsible for maintaining the IT infrastructure and software required to support the data warehouse
- Database administrator (DBA)
  - Responsible for the database that is at the heart of the data warehouse architecture
- Architect
  - Designs the technical roadmap, from end-to-end, for the implementation
- Modeler
  - Performs data modeling and is responsible for designing the star schema, as well as logical and physical design
- Developers
  - Can be experts in various technologies including databases, ETL, report development, etc.
- ETL developer
  - Plans, designs, and develops the ETL process
- Front-end developer
  - Develops reports, queries, and dashboards
- Back-end developer
  - Performs back-end development tasks including OLAP development (cube development, etc.)

In many cases, a single resource performs multiple tasks, such as architect and data modeler, or front-end and back-end development.

344 What are the benefits of performing skills assessment?

Before project team members are selected, there should be a skills assessment exercise. The skill levels and capabilities of the potential project team members and ultimate end-users need to be determined. Both technical and business skills assessments must be performed. The skills assessment exercise helps pinpoint deficiencies and indicates the areas where external resources may be required for implementation and/or providing support after the data warehouse becomes operational.

345 Why should an experienced leader be chosen as the project leader?

A project leader/manager must be experienced in implementing data warehouse or enterprise application projects, must understand the business as well as technology, and must have excellent project management skills. A project manager with these qualities will be able to implement important policies and procedures, closely manage and control the project, quickly identify risks and initiate mitigation strategies, and provide leadership throughout the project, especially when major issues arise.

346 How critical is the selection of the project leader?

Good project management can make the difference between a successful and a failed data warehouse implementation. The implementation leader should be one who possesses the qualities associated with a successful project manager. The person selected for such a position should have a reputation for completing projects on time and within budget. The project manager should be a decisive leader who must be given adequate authority, so that the project does not suffer due to the lack of adequate decision-making authority.

347 What happens when a project is led by uninformed resources?

Projects have been implemented by uninformed project leaders, who did not even understand the fundamental differences between a database and a data warehouse; these projects did not finish on time or on budget, or they failed completely. In many such cases, these project leaders finally did learn the differences but, unfortunately, it was too late to make a difference to lead the project to a successful completion.

348 Which data warehouse resource skills are in short supply?

Data warehousing has evolved and matured in the past decade—from an unproven to an established mainstream technology. Although the professionals required to implement data warehouse projects are available in large numbers at this time, it is still difficult to find key resources when needed. In particular, there is a shortage of experienced project managers and data warehouse architects, or designers, who can translate an organization's business requirements into a technical architecture that can be implemented efficiently and optimally.

349 Why should project resources be dedicated?

Some organizations use the same resources for production support as well as an implementation (or enhancement) project. Since production problems can be unexpected and the time required to fix them can vary, resources assigned simultaneously to production support and projects have a difficult time remaining focused and completing their project deliverables on time. Also, typically, the mindset and attitude of those working on fixes differs from those who work on projects. Hence, whenever possible, different resources should be used for production support and projects.

350 Why must specific responsibilities and deliverables be assigned?

The roles and responsibilities on a data warehouse project should be assigned clearly. Wherever possible, specific project tasks with corresponding responsibilities should be assigned to individual team members; this ensures ownership and proper monitoring. The deliverables for each phase, and for important project milestones, should be assigned to individual resources—employees as well as consultants.

351 Which approaches can be used to implement a project with partners?

Three common approaches are used for implementing a data warehouse:

- Using in-house staff
- Using a vendor
- Teaming with a partner

Unless resources within the organization have data warehouse or data mart implementation experience, the first option can mean a longer implementation time and considerably higher risk in terms of cost and time. The lack of technical know-how can lead to a flawed design, poor performance, extraction and loading problems, selection of the wrong tools, and other technical issues.

In the second option, with an experienced vendor, the implementation can be faster and smoother. Maintaining the system can be an issue after the vendor leaves, however, because of inadequate knowledge transfer to the operational staff. Therefore, upgrading such a system will be more expensive compared with a system implemented by in-house staff. Also, there will be a greater need for ongoing and future consulting/training costs.

Typically, the third approach is the best because a skilled consulting partner implements the data warehouse in close collaboration with company employees, who pick up both business and technical skills. The consulting partner, who must be reliable and competent, must be selected carefully through a well-established screening and evaluation process. Failure to select the right implementation partner can be a very costly mistake. An important consideration in the selection process is to determine whether the partner, besides designing and implementing the data warehouse, can also provide ongoing support, if required.

352 Should consultants be used extensively for implementing projects?

The use of consultants for data warehouse projects is required when in-house expertise is lacking or unavailable, which happens quite frequently. However, this has been counterproductive when, because of the unavailability of key employees and the requirement to rush a project, there has been excessive use of consultants. In such cases, limited knowledge transfer takes place and, consequently, there is prolonged dependency on consultants. Therefore, although consultants should be used, such use should be exercised with care so that it does not turn out to be counterproductive.

CHAPTER 36

PROJECT DEFINITION AND INITIATION

353 What is the trigger for a data warehouse project?

The trigger for a data warehouse project typically originates from senior management, who realize that there is a severe need for information that can enable the organization to improve its performance. However, there are many other reasons or scenarios that can trigger the project, including the following, each of which points to a potential data warehouse solution:

- Lack of integrated information required for decision making
- Critical analysis, strategic or operations not available when required
- Data and results not trusted—one version of the truth desired
- Push for growth
- Need to manage costs
- Information infrastructure falling apart and unmanageable
- Improved analytical capabilities of competition causing problems
- Increased awareness as a result of sales pitch by business intelligence vendor

354 What is involved in defining the problem?

At this stage, after the problem has been recognized and the trigger has initiated the process, the first step is taken to solve the problem: defining the problem. This involves asking some fundamental questions—the answers will help define the strategy for implementing a solution.

355 What types of questions need to be answered in order to define the problem?

Following are questions that need to be asked in order to determine the problem and identify *potential* solutions:

- What are the *specific* problems?
  - Which are the most pressing?
  - Which can be resolved by implementing either a data warehouse solution or another technology?
  - What are the core business processes, as well as organizational units, that have these issues?
- What are the criteria for measuring success?
  - Criteria need to be defined, because they will be used to determine whether various solutions (including a data warehouse), can meet or exceed them.
- What are the KPIs and metrics for each strategic initiative?
  - Will performance metrics improve if there is enhanced access to information? How much?
- What are the key strategic initiatives?
- Will a data warehouse solve the problem(s)?
  - The answer could be positive, or there might be an indication that other technologies would be better able to solve the problem. This question might be answered internally or by a consulting partner hired for this purpose.
- Is building the data warehouse the only option?
  - Can the problem be solved by using Web-based solutions?
  - Is software as a service a potential solution?

- What is the timeline?
    - How fast is the resolution of the problem desired?
    - What is driving the desired schedule?
    - Which of the various solutions can be implemented within the desired timeline?
- How much money can be allocated for resolving this problem?
    - The amount of funding will determine what type of solution can be considered—such as an off-the-shelf solution—as well as the scale of the project. Funding limitations might rule out an EDW. In that case, the question to be asked is whether a phased data mart solution could be a potential solution.
- What types of resources are available?
    - What type of solutions can be implemented with the available internal resources and budget?
    - Can some aspects, such as development, be outsourced?

After the questions have been formulated, a small team is formed to perform an initial assessment of the data warehouse project.

356 What is the project definition phase?

In this phase, the idea for implementing a data warehouse takes shape, leading to the project initiation phase.

357 Which tasks are performed in the project definition phase?

In this project phase, a number of tasks are performed. The first is to assess the readiness of the organization to undertake a project of such magnitude. In the next step, the high-level preliminary scope for the project is developed. The scope is determined to a large degree by the reporting objective, analytical versus operational, and how much additional information and functionality is to be provided to those who will gain access to the new system. The processes for which the data warehouse will be implemented are also identified in this phase.

At this stage various options are also presented, such as implementing a pilot or dividing the project into smaller projects with a phased roll-out.

The next step involves creating a preliminary project plan (or plans, if multiple options are to be considered), and compiling high-level preliminary cost estimates. The cost estimates will be made for one or both options—top-down and bottom-up. The functional areas to be covered are identified, together with the subject areas to be implemented for satisfying their needs. Based on this information, the high-level plan, with a preliminary schedule, is created. The plan contains high-level estimates for various tasks, especially requirements-gathering and ETL, because they require the maximum time and effort.

358 What other tasks are performed in the project definition phase?

The data warehouse initiative is a very expensive undertaking and should be justified through a cost/benefit analysis. Therefore, one of the activities during the project initiation phase is to perform business case analysis and justification for which the inputs include high-level requirements, estimates of costs and benefits, risks, and alternative solutions. The outcome of this exercise is an estimate of the potential return on investment. This exercise provides only an estimate because, at this stage, it is difficult to predict precisely the magnitude of benefits that can accrue upon the implementation of a data warehouse; however, using numbers available to industry experts, a reasonable estimate can be generated. For this task, it makes sense to involve an experienced consultant or a professional consulting company that has extensive business intelligence implementation experience.

Finally, important resources that should or must be involved in the project are identified in this phase, though approval and their actual allocation to the project are done later.

359 Who provides approval for the initiation phase?

After the project definition phase, with the preliminary project scope and approach having been determined, the next step involves obtaining approval for the next phase—project initiation. The approval of the business case is provided by the project sponsor(s). The business owner and IT sponsor are also required to approve the business case before the project proceeds to the next phase.

360 What is the project initiation phase?

The project initiation phase provides the first assessment and estimate of the data warehouse scope, cost, and schedule. These are arrived at after prioritization of the high-level business requirements and business performance goals. For example, the goals can be to minimize cost, maximize profits, integrate customer data to improve customer satisfaction, increase productivity, increase service renewals, introduce analytical capabilities to a particular division, and so forth. Depending on how they are prioritized, the processes and functional areas to be selected for implementation will vary, which can impact the scope, cost, and schedule.

In addition to the prioritization that is performed from the business perspective (that is to say, by the business stakeholders), another exercise is also executed in this stage: determining the feasibility of implementing the solution for each of the prioritized items, together with their potential cost and schedule.

361 What other tasks are executed in the initiation phase?

At this stage, the project management structure is setup. The project manager is identified who, along with the project sponsor, starts to identify business process owners and potential senior project team members. After most of the project team members have been identified, the project team's kick-off meeting is organized. At this meeting, the team members are introduced and the highlights of the project are communicated to them. The information communicated includes the project structure, implementation scope, high-level plan, milestones, criteria for measuring success, as well as roles and responsibilities.

The communication plan, which is a key element of every major project, is developed in this phase. It is basically a plan for disseminating communications throughout the life of the project, including the types of reports to be developed, the schedule of meetings, and communication targets.

At this stage, various processes are developed to manage change requests, issues and risks, escalation processes, data quality, governance, sign-offs, and other particulars. Also finalized are the metrics for determining success, such as cost reduction, increase in revenue and/or productivity, and reliability improvement.

CHAPTER 37

PROJECT PLANNING

362 When is the data warehouse project plan created?

After the approval has been obtained, the project planning begins. During this phase, the preliminary schedule for the data warehouse project is set, which provides the timeframe during which the project has to be implemented. The specified timeframe becomes the basis for the detailed project plan, which includes activities, durations, dependencies (predecessor/successor activities), and deliverables, as well as assignment of internal and external resources to specific tasks. The project plan, once developed, will confirm whether the project can be delivered per the desired time frame. Besides helping to manage the project, the project plan documents what is to be expected and who is to meet those expectations—business, IT, and individuals assigned to the project.

363 What are the phases in a typical data warehouse project?

A data warehouse implementation project is defined by the following phases:

- Planning
    - In addition to the typical planning tasks, this phase also includes the setup of the physical environment.
- Analysis
    - In this phase, the business is analyzed and requirements-gathering is performed.

- Design
  - Tasks in this phase include data modeling, cube design, extraction, transformation, and loading.
- Development
  - In this phase, the data warehouse is constructed per the design; the procedures include report development, dashboard development, query optimization, and unit testing; security is also implemented.
- Testing
  - In this phase, quality assurance tasks are performed and UAT is performed to validate the reports and queries.
- Deployment
  - In this phase, the data warehouse is rolled out to the users.
- Operation and maintenance
  - After go-live, the data warehouse is operated as a production unit; over time, enhancements are implemented, per the change management process.

364 Which factors influence costs?

The costs associated with a data warehouse project can be influenced by a large number of variables. The following are key items that can impact the cost significantly:

- Scope
- Schedule
- Approach
- Architecture
- Infrastructure—current and planned
- Database size
- Source data characteristics and complexity
- Source data quality

- Number and types of users
- Complexity of tools
- Cost of tools
- Proprietary or open-source tools
- Implementation approach (internal or with a partner)
- Training

365 How important is the data warehouse project plan?

Whereas project management is essential for operational projects, it is critical for data warehouse projects, which are unique; they are less defined than OLTP projects, and have more risks associated with them. For many project team members, the iterative and unique nature of the project, and the way it is implemented, is completely new. For them, as well as for experienced team members, the project plan is a very important tool that can enable them to work effectively and discharge their responsibilities. A good project plan ensures that all team members are driving toward the same goal at the same pace. It provides project management with the tool that is critical for monitoring and controlling the project. Without a project plan, the probability of project failure is extremely high.

366 What is the impact of an inadequate project plan or inaccurate estimates?

A data warehouse project must always be implemented according to a realistic project plan in order that the project can be effectively monitored, controlled, and completed. A project will fail if the costs for various systems, and the time required to implement various activities, are not accurately estimated. A project that is estimated inaccurately will invariably fail because of cost overruns and delays.

367 Why should a scope agreement be reflected in the project plan?

The scope agreement is a document that specifies, for the business users, the deliverables—the functionality and data—that IT will enable by the end of the project. It also specifies what will be excluded, schedule, responsibilities, and other relevant information. The document details the expectations for IT as well as for the business. The scope document forms the basis for determining whether the project was delivered as specified and, also, how it should be classified—failed or successful.

368 What is the impact of scope changes on the schedule?

Most projects receive requests for changes to requirements at various stages. These can be minor tweaks, enhancements, or brand new functionalities. In data warehouse projects, these requests can be wide ranging, such as adding an additional process, subject area, source, historical data, reports, dashboards, data sources, column in a report, new dimension or fact, delivery method, security, and others. Some requests can be incorporated with little measurable effort. Some requests perhaps seem very simple but can have an unintended impact that can create serious issues impacting the schedule and/or cost. Sometimes, even though it might not be realized when requested, a change request can risk the project or particular deliverables.

369 Why does scope change in data warehouse projects?

The initial data warehouse objectives are often general, rather than precise, statements. Therefore, business analysis often leads to refinements and changes in requirements and, consequently, the scope. Because data warehouse implementations are characterized by an iterative approach, requirements are often refined as initial assumptions and design are revisited because of subsequent observations and discoveries. Therefore, scope change can occur quite a few times during the project life cycle. The key is to minimize and control the scope changes.

370 What is included in the infrastructure plan?

The project plan includes an infrastructure plan component. It contains the procurement and installation activities relevant to the physical infrastructure required to support the data warehouse implementation. It includes the hardware, software, network, and tools required for that purpose, such as servers, database, monitoring software, and front-end tool.

371 What is included in the resource plan?

The project plan has to be executed by resources, which need to be staffed for that purpose. The resource plan includes details about the types of resources required, their desired skill sets, number of resources required for each type of functional or technical skill, schedule and duration of each resource; specific recommendations for resourcing internally or externally can also be included.

372 Where do users need to be involved?

The earlier in the plan users are involved, the better. Data warehouse projects have failed because users did not follow the plan after rollout because of a number of reasons, such as missing or incorrect functionality, incorrect results, unacceptable user interface, poor performance, and politics. There have been fewer issues in projects that involved end-users right from the outset. Therefore, users should be involved in every phase where they can provide input and feedback such as initial scoping, requirements-gathering, data validation, mock-ups during development, reports and dashboard testing, UAT, and other details.

373 What is included in the design and development plans?

In this component of the project plan, activities relevant to the design and development phases of the data warehouse implementation are included. Such activities include data modeling, creating connections to source systems, creating fact tables, creating dimension tables, individual ETL tasks, development in various environments (sandbox, development, QA, and production), unit testing, as well as many other associated technical activities.

374 What is included in the testing plan?

In the testing plan, various activities associated with testing are included. The specific activities include testing each report and dashboard, which are selected for that purpose. The testing will ensure that the results are correct, all required fields are present, totals and subtotals match, look and feel is acceptable, access method works and is acceptable, security works as expected for every profile, and so forth.

The testing activities are performed by SMEs, end-users, power users, and members of the QA team, if such a dedicated team is organized. The formal testing procedure is known as the User Acceptance Test. The last activity in this plan is the sign-off, which occurs if the UAT Lead is satisfied that the system performs as expected.

375 What is included in the training plan?

Training is one of the most important factors that can determine the success of the project. No data warehouse can be considered successful unless its users know how to use the system. Frequently, training is not accorded the importance it should, with very negative consequences.

The training plan details the specifics of the training that is to be delivered. The plan includes initial training for the project team (if a new reporting tool is being introduced), followed by training of a selected group of power users from the business. The end-user training typically covers two components:

- Tool training, which is focused on how to access and use the front-end tool
- Data training, which focuses on the data model, data, and the specifics of the implementation as it impacts the users from the data and reporting perspective

In the last phase, the details for the mass rollout to the end-user community are included. The schedule is based on a number of factors such as phased or mass rollout, number of users, dispersion of the user community across different locations and geographies, and types of reports (ad hoc or canned) being rolled out.

376 What is included in the deployment plan?

After development has been completed and appropriate testing has been performed by the technical and business teams for the ETL and the front-end, the data warehouse can be rolled out into production. The rollout is carried out according to a deployment plan, which contains a list of individual tasks and activities to be executed in a specific sequence, because of various task dependencies.

The deployment tasks span a broad range of activities, such as readying user desktops, portal rollout (for Web-based access), sending out communications to users, activating the Help Desk or Support system, allocation of support responsibilities, activation and communication of login and authorization information, training, confirming readiness, deactivating legacy systems, and deactivating legacy reporting tool (if planned).

377 Is it necessary to develop a communication plan?

Communication is essential if the project team and the users are to be kept informed. When the new system is rolled out, it should not come as a surprise to the users. They need to be informed about the progress of the project and how it will impact them. For the project team members, it is also a useful mechanism for knowing what is happening outside their own area and becoming aware of the bigger picture. It also communicates the project status and helps quell any rumors, which tend to disproportionately highlight problems with the project. Therefore, a communication plan must be included in every data warehouse project.

CHAPTER 38

ANALYSIS

378 What is the business discovery process?

The basic analysis starts with the business discovery process; this involves comprehending the environment in which the business is operating, gathering and documenting the business requirements, and identifying gaps through a process known as gap analysis. The results of this exercise provide the input for the subsequent project tasks and phases.

379 Why should the business environment be studied?

Understanding the business environment will ensure that the data warehouse, when implemented, will support the business requirements and processes. Only a comprehensive study of the environment can enable business and technical assumptions to be made that are valid and, therefore, do not cause issues and rework to be performed at a later stage. At the top of the list of items to be determined are the business objectives or goals. For example, the business objective can be "The business intelligence system must support the strategic analysis of revenue and costs, as well as improve customer satisfaction."

Some of the key investigations in this phase include determining the major initiatives planned or in progress, identifying key players—the decision makers, potential barriers, problems and pain points, users of the existing and proposed system(s), prior history of attempts to solve the problems, relationship between IT and the business, and IT strengths and weaknesses.

380 Which items are determined during the analysis?

Some of the important items that are typically determined or defined in the analysis phase include the following:

- Pain points
- Existing as well as planned platforms and processes
- Impact on existing infrastructure (hardware, software, networks, etc.) and personnel
- Mandatory and desired features and functions
- Subject areas (customers, orders, sales, bookings, etc.)
- Query and reporting requirements
- Range of queries expected
- Data requirements—which data is required to be moved into the data warehouse (customers, bookings, sales, external data, etc.)
- Data sources and elements (legacy and other sources—external or internal)
- Primary data source when data is available in multiple sources
- Data levels (detailed versus summarized, granularity)
- Data flows—how the sources, OLTP systems/other data marts/EDW feed the data warehouse
- Frequency of data loading into the data warehouse
- Historical data requirements
- Dimensional business model (facts, dimensions, hierarchies, and relationships)
- Logical data model
- Business rules to be used to integrate data from multiple sources
- Business rules for aggregation
- Rules for fixing/dealing with missing or dirty data
- Sizing

381 How does requirements-gathering differ for data warehouse vs. OLTP systems?

In an OLTP system, the requirements are determined through various well-known techniques; they are documented and then implemented through a conventional IT project using a proven methodology such as the Waterfall method. The nature of a data warehouse project, however, is different because of the wide range of business and process functionalities that can be implemented, the steady stream of requests for enhanced functionality and data, and because of its iterative nature. In data warehouse projects, requirements are refined periodically as more information comes to light during the analysis and design phases.

Frequently in a data warehouse project, after an initial demo and presentation of mockups, the business users demand changes. This forces the requirements to be revisited and the requested changes, if accepted, are incorporated in the scope of work to be performed. The design is then modified as required, and the requirements are implemented.

It is rare for the initial requirements to be implemented without changes. Hence, after the initial requirements have been elicited and documented, any additional or modified requirements should be incorporated only after they have been approved, following their submission to a scope and change control process.

382 What is determined during the requirements-gathering phase?

The requirements to be gathered in this phase of the project are quite comprehensive. Anything that can be considered important for meeting the information needs of the users and the data warehouse implementation is a target for investigation. In general, the "As-Is" environment is first investigated. This is followed by determining the environment that is desired after the implementation, i.e., the "To-Be" environment. The following list indicates the types of information that is typically gathering during this phase:

- Key business initiatives
- Role of business units in the strategic initiatives

- Key IT projects
- Business structure and organization
- Objectives of the business units
- Department objectives
- Profitability of the business entities
- Criteria for measuring performance
- KPIs and other metrics
- Roles and responsibilities
- Anticipated usage of the new data warehouse system
- Processes/subject areas of highest interest
- Need for real-time information
- Types of static reports
- Strategic and operational reports
- Analytical requirements
- Data sources and their location
- Historical data sources and availability
- Data structures
- Data quality
- Data elements
- Data extraction procedures
- Dimensions
- Aggregates
- Attributes
- Hierarchies (organization, products, sales, geographical, etc.)
- Business rules
- Reporting in local and global currencies

- Information delivery mechanisms
- Delivery frequency
- Previous database upgrade
- Previous operating system upgrade
- Previous network upgrade
- Status of overall infrastructure
- Open-source software and applications
- Cloud-based initiatives
- Protocols and data connection supported
- User locations (LAN, WAN, VPN, Internet, mobile devices)
- Type of IT support
- Competition

383 Who is involved in the requirements-gathering phase?

The business requirements are collected through various requirements-gathering techniques and include the following participants:

- Executives
- Managers (line and department)
- DBA
- IT managers
- Business analysts
- System analysts
- SMEs
- Report developers
- Architect and/or data modelers
- Staff supporting current reporting applications

384 What are the requirements-gathering methods?

There are many requirement gathering techniques used in data warehousing projects:

- Review of corporate strategic documents
- Review of corporate and business performance guideline documents
- Review of business/process documents
- Review of existing IT documentation
- Review of report specifications (for existing reports)
- One-on-one interviews
- Group interviews
- Joint Application Development (JAD) sessions
- Questionnaires
- Workshops

385 What should be done if the requirement changes are significant?

At the end of the requirements-gathering exercise, it will become apparent if the initial assumptions, made during the project definition phase, were valid. If the assumptions are incorrect and it appears that the scope/schedule will be impacted by the discoveries made during the requirements-gathering phase, the changes must be presented to the sponsor or Steering Committee for review and approval. After approval, as required, necessary changes are made to the scope, cost, and schedule.

386 What are requirements-gathering issues and challenges?

The requirements-gathering phase is one of the longest ones in the data warehouse implementation cycle. There are many issues and challenges associated with it:

- Key people not assigned to attend interviews or workshops
- Key resource left, creating an information gap

- Availability of key resources for the interviews
- Incomplete information provided and multiple sessions required
- Casual approach by the participants
- Users unknowledgeable or confused
- Conflicting responses
- Conflicting priorities
- Confusing needs with wants
- Blanket requests (such as requesting all available historical data)
- Unwillingness to release or share data
- New system is perceived to be a threat
- Lack of confidence in the data warehouse project
- Creating the appropriate questionnaires
- Lack of available documentation
- Politics

CHAPTER 39

ANALYSIS: ADDITIONAL TOPICS

387 How can the data environment be analyzed?

The data environment needs to be studied during the requirements-gathering exercise, because it can impact the design and development in many ways. Following are the key items that need to be evaluated in order to ensure that data, which is the lifeblood of a data warehouse, can be moved efficiently and effectively into its new home:

- Selection of the data sources
- Data volumes
- Business rules
- Data acquisition
- Data extraction
- Data transformation
- Data loading
- Technology to be used for moving data
- Technology for connecting applications
- Protocols and data connection supported
- Data cleansing
- Data validation
- Access approach
- Network infrastructure

- Peak and normal network traffic throughput
- Database
- Data storage
- Data traffic
- Data refresh strategy
- Historical data requirements
- External data requirements
- Archiving requirements
- Shared data
- Two-way data flow

388 What is the objective of gap analysis?

The objective of gap analysis, during business requirements analysis, is to identify the areas where specific functionality is currently lacking and can be met by the new system—the data warehouse. The analysis will also identify the gaps that will occur when the new system is unable to provide the desired functionality. After a gap is identified, a decision is made on how to deal with it. There are some typical resolutions for a gap:

- Left unfilled
- Taken care of through a proposed workaround
- Solved by implementing a solution

The solution can be implemented via the data warehouse or an external system, which could entail additional development effort, additional tools or infrastructure, additional cost, and could also impact the schedule.

389 What is a data gap?

Data, for which a data warehouse breathes and lives, is one of the most critical items to be analyzed during the requirements-gathering exercise. The data to be stored in a data warehouse has to meet the business reporting and analytical requirements. Therefore, its availability and condition are the focus of very intense analysis. Based on the gap that is discovered, a determination can be made whether the data available can meet the business requirements. If it is not available, or is dirty, it will be noted as a data gap so that a determination of the time and effort required to cover the shortcoming can be made.

390 What is an infrastructure gap?

The infrastructure required to support the data warehouse also needs to be studied to determine the gaps. The objective is to determine whether it can support the proposed data warehouse infrastructure and architecture. The analysis covers a range of components, including hardware, middleware, servers, application software, operating system, network, connectivity between systems, tools, and RDBMS. At the conclusion of the analysis, the infrastructure gaps are identified, together with potential solutions for rectifying the shortcomings. These solutions are then evaluated and, if approved, are incorporated into the project plan, and steps are initiated to procure and install the required items, as needed.

391 What is a resource gap?

The resource gaps identify constraints pertaining to project personnel skills and the availability of resources based on the proposed schedule and budget. These are identified so that the risk due to the gap and its impact on the project can be evaluated. Also, after review, project management can initiate steps to resolve the gap.

392 What can happen as a result of inadequate or inappropriate requirements?

A data warehouse project will fail, as many have over the years, if the focus is on integrating and providing data to the data warehouse, rather than understanding user needs and requirements. The users' reporting, querying, and analytical needs must be analyzed and determined. If the user needs are not accurately determined and the data warehouse implementation is based on inadequate or inappropriate requirements, failure is assured.

393 What can happen when requirements are unclear and/or changing?

After a project has started with a well-defined scope, requirements, and specific deliverables, no changes must be entertained and implemented unless they are approved through a scope-change control process. Failure to follow this fundamental rule of projects, especially with regard to implementations characterized by unclear or changing requirements, has led to numerous data warehouse project failures.

394 How should initial business requirements be finalized?

After the analysis has been completed and the business requirements have been clearly defined, they must be documented. This ensures that there is no subsequent confusion about what is to be implemented. The requirements are compiled in the Business Requirements Document (BRD), which is signed-off by the business owner(s) as well as IT.

395 What type of end-user reporting requirements need to be determined?

The requirements-gathering exercise is also used to identify the methods used by end-users to access and display data. The exercise involves an analysis of the queries, reports, scorecards, and dashboards being currently used, as well as the available data models. It will reveal the type of analysis being performed (strategic or operational), types and frequency of reports executed (daily/weekly/monthly/quarterly/annual), trend and statistical analysis, roles from the reporting perspective, and data and report security requirements.

396 What is covered in the IT infrastructure analysis?

The IT infrastructure evaluation can influence the selection of the various tools, including the front-end tool, database, and OLAP server. The evaluation typically covers the following components:

- IT infrastructure and architecture roadmap
- Installed core system (such as IBM, Oracle, HP)
- Installed ERP system

- Planned ERP system, if any plans exist to switch
- Planned core system
- Upgrade plans for various IT infrastructure components
- Source systems (ERP, CRM, Standalone source systems, etc.)
- Systems planned to be retired
- Databases
- MDM strategy
- Servers (including OLAP and Web servers)
- Operating systems
- Hardware
- Enterprise Application Integration (EAI) systems, if any
- Integration techniques and technologies
- Platforms

397 What type of ETL analysis can be performed?

Although the detailed ETL design is performed during the design phase, a high-level preliminary design for extraction, transformation, and loading can be performed during the analysis phase of the project. This analysis can reveal some complexities at an early stage, which can enable the project plan to be refined by incorporating additional time and effort required as a result of the complexity.

398 What changes can the analysis phase lead to?

The analysis phase leads to the definition of the architecture as well as the processes for linking the data sources, the data warehouse, and the front-end access tools. It can result in increased or decreased scope. If the scope is changed, the project plan will also be updated to reflect the additional, or reduced, time and effort that will be required. The results from this phase also have the potential to impact the implementation approach, top-down or bottom-up, which may or may not have been selected previously.

CHAPTER 40

DESIGN

399 What is the objective of the design phase?

The objective of the design system is to provide a solution that will be optimal from the cost and schedule perspective, within the constraints of the business and technical environment, as well as future operation and maintenance. It aims to translate the business requirements into a solution and determine how the data warehouse can be implemented optimally.

400 What is the data warehouse design objective?

The ultimate aim of the design process is to create a data warehouse loaded with rich data that can be analyzed using analytics, queries, and reports. The objects with which the tools interface are the fact and dimension tables, which are the most important elements that the design process focuses on.

A typical installation will be based on a complex design with numerous sources, data marts, operational data stores (ODS); multiproviders, and other objects connected through a complex relationship. The design architecture can be fairly dynamic and can change over time as a result of additions, enhancements, and changes to objects and flows.

401 Which components are defined in the design phase?

During the design phase, the overall solution is designed and includes the following:

- Database architecture including the data warehouse database, OLAP server, and ODS systems
- Database sizing

- Servers
- Hardware sizing
- Hardware configuration
- Migration architecture for the sandbox, development, QA, production, and training environments
- Extraction process
- Data staging
- Transformation process
- Loading process
- Access tool and mechanism
- Network
- Security and access control
- Backup procedures
- Recovery procedures
- Data model
- Data structures
- Fact tables
- Dimension tables
- Aggregates
- Dashboards
- Alert systems
- Middleware and connectivity
- Data warehouse administration
- Metadata
- Repositories
- Operating system

402 Is the architecture significantly different across projects?

The high-level process, which is similar across most data warehouse projects, contains the basic three components: acquisition, storage, and access. The individual components, such as hardware and tools, are also common. However, the configuration varies across different projects. The primary work is in sizing and designing the different processes and components to work together optimally within the defined architecture.

403 Which inputs are needed for designing the architecture?

The content and size requirements of the following components are a prerequisite for designing the architecture: source data, data staging, data storage, and information delivery. These include numerous subitems such as source systems, operating system, and databases. Additional components that also need to be defined include information delivery, and metadata, as well as administration. The list of variables that define all these items is extensive and includes items such as interfacing applications, data mart or EDW architecture, type of database, open-source or proprietary tools, number of users, dashboards, scorecards, types of analysis, historical and operational data requirements, volume of data to be extracted and stored, data mapping, data cleansing, growth forecast, security, alerts, among others.

404 Who participates in developing a design?

The design is primarily performed by the technical team, though the business is closely involved because they have to provide constant and valuable input. The technical team involves the architect, data modeler, ETL expert, front-end tool developer, source systems expert, and IT representatives, including the DBA. On the business side, the business analyst leads the effort for which support is provided by the functional experts/SMEs and department managers/directors.

405 What is involved in designing an optimal solution?

An optimal design has to be developed, keeping in mind its impact on the project being implemented as well as future operation and maintenance. There is always a conflict between competing priorities and needs. At times, a solution might be very simple to implement but it could cause a nightmare in the future, because of excessive maintenance or performance issues. On the other hand, a complex solution might be perfect for the future but could push the schedule and also have a negative cost impact.

406 What are common variables influencing the design?

The list of potential issues to be addressed and/or resolved during the design phase can be fairly extensive. The following list is just a sampling of the potential items and questions that need attention:

- How much data is to be stored in the data warehouse (months, years)?
- What level of detailed data is to be stored?
- Should the loading frequency be implemented differently for different data sets (real-time and daily)?
- Is the data to be loaded once a day or in real-time?
- Which source system should be used?
- Which data should be aggregated?
- How will data be backed up?
- How will data replication be performed?
- When should the loading jobs be scheduled?
- Which OLAP functionality is desired?
- Which facts should be selected?
- Which fact tables should be constructed?
- Which business dimensions should be selected?
- Should two subject areas be retained or consolidated into one?
- How will hierarchies be implemented?
- What will be the drill-down path?
- Which dimensions can be drilled down by different users?

- Which user, or user group, can drill down various dimensions?
- How will rollups be performed?
- Should there be dedicated QA and training systems?
- Should calculations be precalculated in the back end or performed in the front-end tool?
- How will runaway queries be handled?
- Should an open-source tool be used?
- How will the various tools from different vendors be integrated?

407 Which information delivery components are impacted by requirements?

The requirements can significantly influence many information delivery components. The impact can extend to reports, queries, dashboards, scorecards, delivery mechanism, access, security and authorization, drill-down capabilities, reporting against aggregated data, alerts, and ability to access near-current or real-time data.

408 Which design differences need to be appreciated?

The primary design objective of a data warehouse, with its decision support and analysis requirements, is querying and reporting. A data warehouse is required to respond to complex and ad hoc queries, rather than provide simple reporting. A data warehouse aims to extract information from a database rather than capture and store data. Hence, it places emphasis on analytical tasks such as drill-down capabilities, and slicing and dicing.

On the other hand, an OLTP system's primary objective is to capture and store transaction data, which leads to its performance requirement that the database be updated efficiently. An OLTP system database stores only current operational data, which typically ranges from six months to two years. A data warehouse contains current as well as historical data that increases its size tremendously and, consequently, impacts its performance. It also contains a time element, which makes it more complex.

Most IT personnel are familiar with OLTP systems, because they come from that background. They are frequently unaware, however, of how an OLTP database design differs compared with a data warehouse database. It is important that such resources, new to a data warehouse project, be made aware of the differences as soon as possible so that they can avoid the common pitfalls.

409 What is a common faulty design assumption?

A fairly common and critical mistake made by those implementing their first data warehouse project is their flawed assumption that it is just like an OLTP database project. Since they are unaware of the fundamental design difference between a traditional database and a data warehouse—normalization versus denormalization—they incorrectly assume that a conventional database system has to be designed—a relatively simple task that can be performed by many experienced in-house IT personnel. However, they do not realize until it is too late that data warehousing is a process, encompassing many components and techniques, whose successful implementation requires knowledge of business as well as technology.

410 What is the design impact of conflicting business rules?

The various groups and processes within an organization can have conflicting business rules, which can impact the selection, screening, and import of data from various sources. If the definitions used by different groups are inconsistent, results of calculations can vary, thereby creating many issues. For example, the net sales figure can be different depending on whether returns are included or excluded. If such potential issues are not addressed and resolved in the design phase, inconsistent results in different reports can undermine the credibility of the data warehouse.

411 How do business changes impact design?

No business remains static, and there are changes that an organization can experience that can impact the data warehouse system:

- Mergers
- Acquisitions

- Reorganization of business units
- Organizational and reporting structure changes
- Changes in definitions
- Changes in key figures or dimensions (which can be slow or frequent)
- New metrics

The potential for business and organizational changes needs to be evaluated, and planned for, during the design process.

412 What can the lack of consensus regarding data definitions lead to?

Users must have confidence in the data warehouse data that they access and analyze. If there are any inconsistent results, there can be loss of confidence and, consequently, the warehouse will be less likely to be used. A common problem causing inconsistencies is the delivery of data with unclear definitions. For example, revenue can be defined as "total revenues minus returns" or simply "gross revenue." Unless such definitions are clear, queries will return results that are inconsistent and, consequently, lead to mistakes and unhappy users.

413 How can existing designs be leveraged?

Many business processes, such as financials and procurement, are fairly standardized and follow best practices, although variations do exist across organizations. Therefore, many vendors provide preconfigured models, containing standard reports and associated objects, which users can use "out of the box" or after some minor modifications or tweaks.

SAP provides "Business Content," which can be quickly activated to provide reporting functionality without requiring extensive development. It contains many applications, across many industries, including Financials, Human Resources, Supply Chain Management, CRM, Supplier Relationship Management, and Product Lifecycle Management. The industries supported include automotive, chemicals, healthcare, retail, media, pharmaceuticals, apparel and footwear, and consumer products. Oracle is another vendor that provides a wide range of data warehouse applications that can be used out of the box.

CHAPTER 41

DESIGN: DATA MODELING AND OLAP DESIGN

414 How important are information and data modeling?

This is one of the most critical tasks in data warehouse design. If the design, which is the foundation upon which the solution is constructed, is solid and based on sound principles, it is assured that the data warehouse will perform well and be termed a success. If it is not done properly, however, the consequences can be far reaching and failure is assured. Poor design can lead to several negative issues:

- Poor performance
- Inability to scale
- Maintenance and upgrade difficulties
- Poor reliability
- Lack of acceptance by the users

415 What drives the data design of a data warehouse?

The requirements are the driver for the data warehouse data design. The design involves various tasks, including identifying the data elements required, combining data elements into appropriate data structures, identifying the relationships between various data structures and putting them together.

416 What is involved in data design?

Data is the fuel that drives the data warehouse system. Therefore, data design is one of the most important tasks that must be performed during the design phase. The foundation for data design is the data model, which needs to be developed for the data repositories—the main data warehouse and the staging areas. The data model contains the business dimensions that are used for the analysis. Additionally, it contains the metrics or measures, which the business uses to analyze the business.

The data model ensures that a query can be designed using various combinations of measures and dimensions. An additional task during the design phase is to identify the levels at which the data, detailed and aggregate, will be stored. The data model must be designed to include different structures that are required to support the reporting and analysis—summary or aggregate as well as details. A well-designed data model will ensure that the data warehouse users have access to what they really want to see and work with.

417 What is involved in data modeling?

The data model development is based on the user requirements, which are used to identify the data sources. In the next step, the logical data model is built; this includes entities, attributes, and relationships that characterize a business function. The logical model is used to develop the physical data model, which is used to design the internal schema of the database. The physical data model includes table structures as well as the relationships between tables.

418 What is involved in physical database design?

The high-level data model identifies the major subject areas as well as the relationships between the major subjects. The mid-level data model identifies attributes, groupings of attributes, as well as the relationships of groupings of attributes. The low-level data model, which is ready for physical database implementation, includes the physical characteristics of attributes.

The physical database design involves designing the database, fact and relationship tables (based on the star schema), data denormalization, indexing, and so forth. The data source physical data models are mapped to the physical model of the data warehouse (source to target). There are several data mapping and transformation tasks:

- Defining the sources
- Determining the logic and rules
- Determining the file layouts
- Data formatting and translation; creating the transformation specifications
- Mapping the source(s) to the target

419 What is involved in aggregation design?

Aggregations are used to provide summarized data, such as monthly totals, to users whose primary interest is in analyzing reports at that level. The advantage of using aggregates is that it decreases the time required to process data. If there are no available aggregates, a query will first have to scan all the low-level detailed data—often numbering in the millions of records—perform the rollup calculations, and then present the data. If the relevant aggregate is available, the results will already have been rolled up and, hence, the query will run very fast, because it will have to scan relatively few data records. The negative is that aggregates impact the loading process.

420 What is the role of users in data modeling?

The business users should be actively involved in the modeling task, because they understand the business and know how it should be analyzed. They know which measures and dimensions are needed and in which combinations. They should be involved from the beginning and should also be used to validate the conclusions. Ideally, the process should be led by a business analyst, though IT participation is also required.

421 When is the OLAP component designed?

The OLAP component, which enables the true potential of a data warehouse system to be realized, is located between the data warehouse and the end-user tools. It should be included as part of the overall design because it is an essential component of most data warehouse systems. The OLAP component cannot be designed independent of the data warehouse, because various design issues can impact both the components (data warehouse and OLAP). For example, the design of aggregates impacts both the data warehouse and OLAP. Therefore, aggregate design cannot be performed in a silo and its impact (such as on storage, loading, and updates), on both systems, must be evaluated as part of the overall design.

422 What are the leading OLAP design decisions?

The OLAP design, like that of the data warehouse, is driven by the specified requirements. One of the most important design decisions, when designing the OLAP component, is the selection of the OLAP architecture and storage—MOLAP, ROLAP, or one of the other alternatives. Selection of the architecture drives the storage, which can be in multidimensional format or relational database format. The design is finalized through an iterative process because most users, usually, do not know what they want. Also, they become more demanding as they start appreciating the capabilities of the OLAP tool and, hence, request features and functions that often require an increase in scope. Other issues to be decided are how to optimize the OLAP cube build and load process, as well as its performance.

423 What are other key OLAP design decisions?

A key decision that has to be made during OLAP design concerns calculations. There are a number of ways in which calculations can be performed; these have an impact on the performance. The first method involves using prestored calculations. Different summary levels of data, as well as derived fields, can be stored in OLAP. In the second method, rather than storing the calculations, the calculations are stored in RAM or temporary tables while anticipating the query. In the third method, the calculations are performed when the query is executed, or, in other words, on the fly. The actual method selected for calculations is driven by the type and frequency of the queries as well as technical issues such as data explosion.

424 What is the data explosion issue?

Data explosion is a common problem afflicting OLAP multidimensional databases. This is caused by an excessive number of blank fields, indexes, and aggregations and causes the data size to multiply when data is loaded into OLAP. Other factors contributing to this phenomenon include too many dimensions and a large number of calculated levels for each dimension. When the calculated and derived values start occupying most of the data cube, and storage increases dramatically, the data becomes difficult to use or manage and, consequently, performance takes a severe hit. Data explosion, which is more of an issue for larger databases, can cause explosions whose magnitude is greater than 1:1,000.

425 How can data explosion be prevented?

Many methods can be used to deal with the data explosion problem. One of the techniques used, which has had very limited success, is to use higher performance hardware and processors. This technique is not recommended because other methods are far better and more effective. The methods used to address this issue include the following:

- Improving and using optimal multidimensional structures
- Limiting the number of OLAP dimensions
- Limiting the number of calculated levels for the selected dimensions
- Smart indexing
- Smart aggregation
- Managing the execution of aggregations (in the background)
- Using minimal storage for empty cells, or no storage by using a pointer, through server configuration
- Using compression for blank fields

CHAPTER 42

DESIGN: ADDITIONAL TOPICS

426 What is involved in source-system mapping?

When the data model is developed, it provides the data elements, entities, measures, and dimensions that are required to be populated in the data warehouse. These elements are to be extracted from the source system(s). Therefore, the next step involves identifying the best source system(s) for pulling in the data. This involves analyzing the complexity, quality, and reliability of the data and the system. In the final step, each of the items is mapped. In other words, a determination is made regarding where the data is to be pulled from (the source system) and where it is to be placed (in the target system—the data warehouse).

For the mapping, various ETL tools, such as Informatica, are used. These tools have user-friendly GUIs, which enable mapping to be done easily through a simple drag and drop procedure.

427 How do source types impact design?

The number and variety of sources feeding a data warehouse impacts its design. Consideration has to be given to the types of sources, which can include internal databases, external databases, Internet data, and flat files. They can impact the protocols, amount of customization required, need for extractor(s), extent of modification (of extractors), loading and update rules, implementation time and cost, data quality and verification, and technical skills requirements.

428 How do changing data sources impact design?

The data sources feeding a data warehouse can change over time because of many reasons. The changes can be major or minor, and need to be planned for when the system is designed. Among the most common reasons are mergers, acquisitions, structural modifications because of internal reorganizations, and the rollout of the data mart or data warehouse to more divisions or departments. The changes can impact the data volumes, interfaces, loading process, loading times, communication methods, and so forth. A well-designed system can handle such changes with relative ease.

429 What is involved in data mapping, transformation, and integration?

The data mapping, transformation, and integration tasks include the following:

- Defining the sources
- Determining the logic and rules
- Determining the file layouts
- Formatting and translating data
- Creating the transformation specifications
- Mapping the source(s) to the target

430 What is involved in ETL scheduling?

The ETL process contains many individual steps within each of its three subprocesses—extraction, transformation, and loading. Some are independent tasks, whereas others have dependencies and can start only after another process has been completed. These have to be automated to a large extent, which requires specifying triggers, defining the job flow, and scheduling. For this purpose, various scheduling tools are available.

431 What is the benefit of designing multicubes?

Sometimes, a query requires data that is stored in two or more cubes. There are two ways in which such an issue can be handled. A new cube with all the required measures and dimensions can be created, which will perhaps not be practical because of many issues such as frequency of usage, loading, maintenance, and performance. In such a case, a multicube can be designed. A multicube provides a view of the data in two or more cubes, without actually creating a new physical entity.

432 How does the access method influence design?

The access method influences the data warehouse design as well as implementation because the requirements will be different for conventional desktop access to reports and queries, compared with Web-based access using a simple browser, tablet, or smartphone. The access method can impact query development, functionality, network traffic, processing power, maintenance and support, authorizations, security, and tools.

433 How does the number of users impact design?

The number of users expected to access and use the data warehouse, the type of analysis and queries that they are expected to perform and execute, as well as their geographic distribution impacts the performance and design. They can influence the type of access to be provided (conventional or Web-based), summarization requirements, granularity, authorizations, security, network requirements, and tool selection. They can also influence the rollout plan, which can impact the approach as well as the development plan and, consequently, the design.

434 How does the navigation requirement influence design?

The requirement for navigation and the ability to slice and dice, drill-down, and drill-across can influence data warehouse and OLAP design. The requirement to navigate, via a single or multiple hierarchies, can impact the development effort and performance. The ability to jump, or navigate, from the current query results to another query, can increase the complexity and be an important design consideration depending on how extensively it is implemented.

435 What role does hierarchy play during design?

A hierarchy is a logical structure, a grouped method, for organizing data and displaying characteristics according to individual evaluation criteria. A hierarchy structure is arranged in successive levels, where the elements in the different levels are interdependent. For example, the time dimension hierarchy can be viewed as year > quarter > month > week > day.

Hierarchies form the basis for aggregation and drill-down criteria within reports. They enable users to analyze data at different levels of detail. The hierarchy design has many implications for reporting and analysis and, therefore, is an important design consideration that needs to be studied carefully. Setting up and maintaining hierarchies can be a complex undertaking, especially if they do not remain static.

436 Why is performance an important design consideration?

Performance is one of the most important design considerations. Poor designs can lead to slow and/or inflexible queries, inability to create some types of queries, inability to navigate or drill down, data explosion, as well as create other limitations that can lead to many issues, such as dissatisfied users, overloaded networks, analysis limitations, and sizing issues. In the worst case, dissatisfied users will simply stop using the data warehouse.

437 What is the objective of data partitioning?

Data partitioning is a technique that breaks up data into smaller physical units that can be managed independently. This technique provides greater flexibility in data management for designers and operations personnel. It overcomes the limitations of large physical units, which cannot be easily structured, reorganized, recovered, or monitored. Partitioning enables sequential scanning, if required, as well as ease of indexing. It allows data to be broken up by region, organization, business unit, date, or other parameters, which can be very useful for the purpose of analysis.

438 What are the techniques for enhancing performance?

A number of techniques are used to enhance performance:

- Data clustering
    - Technique in which objects with similar characteristics are clustered or classified into different groups, which can be achieved by physically storing related tables close to each other

- Data arrays
  - A collection of objects or elements, variables or values, usually in rows and columns
- Parallel processing
  - Technique for simultaneously executing multiple operations or tasks, in parallel
- Referential integrity checks
  - Enforces relationships, one-to-many and many-to-many, within a schema
- Initialization parameters
  - List of parameters, and a value for each parameter, is maintained in a text file; adjustment of these parameters can impact the usage of system resources and improve performance
- Summary levels
  - Involves carefully choosing the detail and summary data levels

439 Do authorizations and security have any significant impact on design?

There are many types of users of a typical data warehouse; they are located at various levels in the corporate hierarchy. Their access level and authorizations vary considerably, depending on their roles, the type of data that they have to access, as well as the types of queries and/or analysis that they have to execute or perform.

Implementing authorizations can be a tedious and complex task, depending on the roles, authorization levels, and the objects/reports/data that the users have to access. Because roles are unique, there can be considerable complexity in implementing the task of mapping roles to objects and authorizations. Each role has to be restricted to specific objects and queries and, hence, in its ability to view specific data or execute authorized queries and reports.

440 Why does the refresh strategy play a role in design?

The data in a data warehouse is updated periodically from its various sources. Therefore, the design has to consider the data refresh frequency (daily, real-time, ad hoc, etc.), incremental loading requirement, potential differences in loading frequency for different cubes or at various periods (month and quarter end), and refresh timing (night, day, peak, or off-peak), which can be impacted by the granularity, aggregation, delta uploads, data volume, uptime requirements, and other factors.

441 Why do upgrade plans need to be considered during design?

A data warehouse project never ends as new subjects continue to be added, cubes continue to be built and/or modified, and enhancement requests never stop. Additionally, releases and upgrades continue to roll in at a regular pace. These releases and upgrades can be relevant to the data warehouse system, individual data warehouse components, source systems (such as the ERP source), ETL tool, and database. Hence, any design needs to plan for future changes to the system, which perhaps will not be currently identified.

442 How can the data warehouse architect insulate users from SQL?

Data warehouse databases contain a large number of tables that are characterized by complex relationships. When a query is executed, the tables required to process it are joined selectively to produce the desired result. To use the data warehouse, nontechnical business users do not need to understand the database structure, names of the tables or their relationships, or how to create an SQL query. However, the data warehouse architect has to design a schema that can be presented to the users in an easy-to-understand, nontechnical format that uses business terms. This is a complex undertaking that requires both technical and business knowledge.

443 How can data volume impact performance?

Data warehouse databases are very large, typically and, in some cases, they are huge—in the terabyte or petabyte range. The amount of data, and the process to load it, can impact performance if they are not properly designed. The data stored in data warehouses is fed from many sources, which makes the database structurally complex. If the structure is not optimized, performance suffers. Also, the process to extract, transform, and load data into the data warehouse is very complicated and is influenced by data volumes. Therefore, if these complexities are not given due importance, the design will be less than optimal and performance will suffer.

444 How do database selection and administration impact design?

The database is a critical data warehouse component, which should be selected after a very thorough evaluation. Database selection is influenced by many factors, such as database features, data volume and frequency, scalability, types of queries, ease of management, proprietary or open source, and metadata management. There are as many selection options available as there are many database vendors, open source and proprietary, whose products exhibit features and capabilities that can vary significantly. At one end are Oracle and IBM products, whereas open-source databases represent the other end of the spectrum. There are considerable differences in their reliability, functionality, cost, performance, operation, maintenance, and features. Therefore, selection of the database can have a significant impact on how the data warehouse is designed, implemented, and operated.

CHAPTER 43

DOCUMENTATION

445 How should initial business requirements be documented?

After the business requirements have been gathered, which is a very time consuming and comprehensive task, they must be documented. Without documentation that is signed off by the business and stakeholders, the success of the project can be easily questioned. After the data warehouse has been constructed, challenges and complaints can be expected concerning what has been implemented; memories tend to be short and there can be several misunderstandings with regard to the decisions made during the requirements-gathering exercise.

This problem can be avoided if the requirements are documented and available to be referred to when any questions are raised. The requirements are usually contained in a document that is popularly known as the Business Requirements Document (BRD). Having solid documentation will ensure two things: (1) scope will be controlled and (2) development will be performed as specified.

446 What needs to be included in design documents?

A number of design documents, the foundation upon which the data warehouse is constructed, are created before the start of the build process. The titles of these individual documents, as well as their content, vary from organization to organization. The overall content of these documents is similar, however. The following sections describe some of the commonly used documents and what they typically contain.

Some of these documents are combined into a single BRD at some organizations, whereas other companies prefer to keep separate records. The important point to note is that the content is of consequence and must be captured and documented in order to have a record of the assumptions and logic for implementing a particular solution. It ensures efficient handling of future enhancements and modifications by analysts and developers who perhaps were not involved with the original project.

447 What is the architecture design document?

This document describes the overall, high-level design of the architecture. For example, it can include the following information, which is based on the accounts receivable (A/R), and deductions data mart analysis requirements:

- Overview
- Logical data model
- Data flow
- Creation of one A/R cube and one deduction cube
- Data source /item feed details
- Data loading schedule (i.e., daily for the deductions cube, monthly for the A/R cube)
- Object details
    - Data sources – name, description, granularity, data extraction frequency, fields (with technical name, description and source information), as well as mapping and transfer rules
    - ODS tables – name, description, granularity, extraction frequency, fields (with description and source information), and update rules
    - Cubes – name, description, granularity, extraction frequency, dimensions, key figures, and navigation attributes
- Master data – name, description, extraction frequency, fields (with description and source information), and update rules

    - Multicubes – name, description, granularity, extraction frequency, dimensions, key figures, and navigation attributes
- Object relationship – loading sequence and configuration
- Data load details
- Star schema
- Aggregates

448 What is the design specifications document?

This document contains the design specifications. The information included in this document is more specific and detailed than in the architecture design document. For example, for a cube design, the following information will typically be included in the design document:

- Business overview
- Design approach
- Star schema
- Data flow
- Appropriate and relevant object details such as name, description, technical name, mapped object, source field, source table, characteristics, key figures, navigation attributes, type, length, decimals, units, and data elements for structures such as
    - Data sources
    - ODS tables
    - Cubes
    - Multicubes
- Update rules for ODS and multicubes
- Data-loading details
- Aggregates
- Performance information including details for aggregates, partitions, indexes, and archiving

449 What is the functional specifications document?

This document contains the functional specifications for the proposed development. It will typically document the following information and requirements:

- Business requirements
- Scope
- Risks
- Alternative solutions
- Gaps
- Assumptions
- Flow diagrams
- Operational and maintenance requirements
- Data volume estimates
- Load frequency
- Error-handling procedure
- Security and authorizations
- Integration requirements
- Testing requirements
- Functional test scenarios

450 What is the technical specifications document?

The technical specifications document contains the technical details for implementing the proposed solution, data model, architecture, OLAP design, ETL design, program components, inputs and outputs, program logic flow, program controls, transfer rules, test scenarios, error processing, report specifications, testing, security, etc. Sometimes multiple technical specification documents are developed, with each one focusing on a particular technical aspect.

451 What is the query design document?

This document provides details about the specific report to be built:

- Report objective and description
- Cube
- Global components (shared)
- Local components (query specific)
- Variables, characteristics, and key figures
- Filters
- Free characteristics
- Column and row items (with business rules and any restrictions)
- Exceptions
- Conditions

452 What is the functional report-specifications document?

This document lists the basic requirements of the query or report:

- Priority
- Report type (strategic or operational)
- Report delivery mechanism (desktop, Web, alert, e-mail, portal, etc.)
- KPIs measured with the report
- Results required (fields, key figures, characteristics, hierarchy)
- Filters
- Selection criteria/prompts
- Exceptions
- Conditions
- Report layout

- Report output (Excel, Web, PDF, chart, PowerPoint, table, graph, etc.)
- Report navigation
- Sorts
- Totals and subtotals
- Drill-down and drill-across requirements
- Aggregation requirements
- Roles using this report
- Authorizations
- Scope (local or global)
- Refresh frequency (hourly, daily, weekly, monthly, quarterly, yearly)
- Execution frequency
- Historical requirements

453 What is the data dictionary?

The data dictionary is another document, a central information repository, which is created for data warehouse projects. Its objective is to include wide-ranging information about the data, including its source, use, and format. The content of the data dictionary has three variations and the significance of each depends on the audience. The first variation is meant for the business users; the second one targets the technical users; the third variation is more comprehensive and contains information that is relevant for both the business and technical users.

The data dictionary is often maintained in a spreadsheet and typically includes the following information:

- Element or field name
- Data element definition
- Description
- Field length

- Field type
- Business context it is used in
- Derived or a calculated field
- Calculation details if it is a calculated field
- Business owner
- Source system it is extracted from
- Relevant mapping information

Other information that the technical users might be interested in can include program elements used by the database, system parameters, entity relationships, schema, security and other details.

CHAPTER 44

DEVELOPMENT

454 Which activities precede development?

The physical data warehouse is constructed in this phase, per the specifications and project scope. Before development, various components of the proposed data warehouse system are evaluated and selected, based on a timeline specified in the project plan. Some components could already be installed within the existing IT infrastructure whereas others, including hardware and software, might need to be procured

455 What is involved in development?

The physical data warehouse, the database that will hold all the imported source data, is created from the logical and physical database designs in a number of steps:

- Data extraction
- Transformation
- Staging
- Loading
- Validation
- Testing

The development and testing activities performed in this phase include some or all of the following:

- Providing the connections between the data warehouse and associated systems, including the source systems

- Mapping to source systems
- Converting data
- ETL and any custom coding of extraction programs
- Creating cubes
- Creating ODS
- Creating reports and queries
- Integrating the data warehouse with the portal, if required
- Creating authorizations

456 Which tasks precede ETL?

An important activity that precedes ETL is the development of programs that perform a variety of tasks:

- Normalizing and building tables
- Modifying/refreshing the warehouse
- Extracting, transforming, and loading data
- Summarizing and aggregating data

457 When are the mappings defined?

The process is started by identifying the scope of the conversion, because all the data available cannot and should not be converted. This is followed by identifying the data sources from which the data will be pulled. In the next step, the destination is identified, together with the conversion technology required to connect the two systems and move the data.

The next step is the most critical—defining the mappings. The transformations and business rules required to be implemented are identified in this step. They provide the basis on which development estimates can be derived. All these steps must be included in the project plan so that every resource is assigned specific responsibilities.

458 What is cutover?

Cutover refers to the activities that are involved in switching from one system to another. In a data warehouse implementation, prior to the system going live, data from the source systems has to be loaded in a particular sequence because of dependencies. For example, all the vendors are loaded first, followed by purchase orders, a week prior to the go-live date. However, during that one-week period, business will not be shutdown and new purchase orders will continue to be generated. There could also be activities associated with open purchase orders, such as a goods receipt against an existing purchase order, or an invoice might be paid. Other activities will also continue, such as the addition of a new vendor in the old system.

All such transactions and changes to master data will need to be captured. Therefore, activities such as these are included in the cutover plan, which lists all the tasks required, in the proper sequence, to switchover to the new data warehouse system. The cutover plan includes all major activities including tasks, schedule, data conversion and loading sequence, and data validation. The cutover plan can be executed over a period that can range from a few days to a few weeks.

459 When is the reporting front-end tool installed?

The reporting tool is installed during the development phase. The access and presentation can vary considerably because users can be dispersed geographically and might access the data warehouse differently, via desktops, laptops, smartphones, portals, Intranet, or the Internet. The front-end installation complexity and customization requirements can vary significantly because there are numerous front-end options, which involve the use of scripting languages as well as off-the-shelf products. A factor to consider, when choosing the options, is flexibility to adjust to back-end server and operating system changes.

460 What is involved in query and report development?

During the development phase, a number of starter reports and queries are created by the development team with some power users, if they are available and have the report-development skills for the selected front-end tool. Most of them are static reports that can be accessed via the portal or through a hyperlink provided to the users. Typically, the critical reports, as well as some dashboards and scorecards, are developed during the development phase.

The objective of a data warehouse is to provide more flexibility for report development and thereby free IT from developing reports and queries that are not complex. Therefore, a minimum number of reports are developed during this phase, because it is expected that the business users will start developing their own reports once they grow accustomed to the new system.

461 Which report options need to be configured?

Although a significant report and query development effort is performed by the business users, the development team has to perform some development work, in the back-end tool, which will enable the report development in a controlled environment. Following is a list of some of the key items that they have to configure:

- View authorization
    - This involves specifying both the users and the data and reports they are allowed to access. For example, supply chain users will not be allowed to view financial data. Similarly, most users will be restricted from viewing data that only senior executives are allowed to access.
- Development authorization
    - This pertains to the authorizations for creating new queries or modifying existing ones and is determined by the roles that are assigned to individual users.
- Filters
    - This pertains to the filters that are applied, either at the back end or in the front end, in reports and dashboards. The users will be able to slice and dice using different filters, which could possibly have default values populated when they are initially executed.

- Roles
  - Depending on the role, the reports or data that a user is able to view, access, modify, or distribute can be configured.
- Distribution
  - Customization will enable or prevent distribution of reports and alerts to individuals or groups of users.
- Customization
  - Depending on a user's location, currency can be customized so that it defaults to the local currency.

462 What are basic query execution guidelines?

If the performance of queries is poor, it can lead to many issues. There can be many reasons for a query to run slow, ranging from poor design to requests for too much unnecessary data. Although there are many back-end solutions and optimization techniques that can be implemented by the development and/or maintenance teams, there are a few actions that the business report developers and users can perform to ensure that queries do not create performance problems.

A basic rule is to retrieve the least volume of data. For example, instead of pulling all the sales data for all the years/periods and then performing a filter on the current year, it makes more sense to plan the query and apply the filter up front, so that only the current year's data is retrieved; this approach can significantly improve performance in many cases. Another tip, when creating reports, is to include only the dimensions and metrics that are actually required for analysis. Also, aggregates should be used wherever possible. Calculations should be performed in the back-end, rather than the front-end, tool. When designing a dashboard, limit the number of KPIs, per best practices, and the number of reports that are to be displayed.

463 How are queries optimized?

Queries can be optimized through various techniques:

- Indexing
- Aggregation

- Denormalizing
- Partitioning (horizontal and vertical)
- Back-end (server) tuning
- Bitmap filtering
- Parallel execution
- Serial and parallel SQL statement tuning
- Utilizing database resource manager
- Optimizing storage requirements
- Minimizing resource consumption

CHAPTER 45

TESTING AND TRAINING

464 What is the purpose of testing?

Testing is used to confirm that the system has been built as specified and that it returns results as expected. As part of this effort, various components and processes are tested, including source data that is loaded into the data warehouse, transformations and calculations, and report results that are output. The back-end testing is performed by the technical/development and quality assurance (QA) teams. The front-end testing, including UAT, is performed by the business users and business analysts, who are supported by the QA team members.

465 For which environment is testing performed?

The testing is performed for each of the following environments:

- Development
- QA
- Training
- Production

However, the level of rigorous testing will vary, with most of the formal testing being performed in the QA box, where the UAT is performed.

466 What is a test plan?

Data warehouse testing is based on a test plan that describes the process for testing. The plan is executed according to test cases that describe the objective and specifics of the individual tests to be performed. The test plan is developed by the testing lead, whereas the test cases are developed by the business/functional users and members of the QA team. The individual test cases list the specific steps to be executed, in the proper sequence, along with the expected results.

467 What are the different types of testing?

There are five types of testing that are performed on a data warehouse to ensure that a high-quality system, which will not cause any issues in the production system, has been developed:

- Unit testing
  - These are single isolated tests that are executed by developers and/or business analysts for some basic checking during the development phase. Unit testing precedes testing by the QA team.
- Integration testing
  - This involves testing a complete process or scenario, from end-to-end, focusing on data flows. This is performed by the business analysts and the QA team.
- Regression testing
  - After an error discovered during unit or integration testing is fixed, re-testing or revalidation is performed to confirm that the problem has been fixed and that the system, function, and/or query works properly.
- Performance testing
  - Performance tests are designed to demonstrate that the system can perform as expected under varying data-loading conditions. The tests, which validate performance under both heavy and peak data loads, also test the performance of various processes such as extraction and transformation.
- User Acceptance Testing
  - Formal testing by the users is known as User Acceptance Testing (UAT); this is described in a subsequent section.

468 What are the tests performed by business users?

In order to determine accuracy, usability and performance, there are three types of tests performed by the functional business users:

- Accuracy
  - The results returned by the system must be accurate. This involves functional testing, which ensures that the function accords to the specified functional requirements.
- Usability
  - The data warehouse system, for those who use the system, should be easily usable. In this type of test, the users interact with the system to check its usability.
- Performance
  - The system should perform at levels that are acceptable to all types of users, including heavy-duty users.

469 How is testing planned and executed?

Typically, testing is done in a controlled QA environment, separate from the development and production systems, and is based on a test plan. The QA system is loaded with data, and the individual objects, reports, queries, and dashboards are developed there, mirroring their development in the development box. Security and authorizations, though not always, are also implemented so that the system reflects what will finally be rolled out in the production system.

470 What is the impact of inadequate testing and validation?

Inadequate testing and validation can cause problems in two ways. First, the ETL effort can require additional work as a result of extraction, transformation, or loading failures, which can potentially impact the cost and schedule. Second, if the data being imported into the data warehouse is not cleansed and validated, it can lead to various issues associated with lack of data integrity. For example, queries can generate incorrect or inconsistent results and, consequently, lead to loss of confidence among users who will be reluctant to use it.

471 What is the role of quality assurance?

After development is completed, the QA team takes over. Their responsibility is to test various aspects of the new system and confirm that it works as specified. The testers test individual reports, queries, scorecards, and dashboards. Typically, they validate the results against reports that run against the existing system. The layout (i.e., look and feel), of the reports is reviewed to confirm that they meet the specifications. The security authorizations are also validated to confirm that users are unable to access data and reports for which they are not authorized.

The QA team consists of dedicated and experienced testers, as well as functional users who know the business and processes quite well and, therefore, can easily pick up errors and discrepancies. Only after the QA team signs off can the system be put into production.

472 What is UAT?

User Acceptance Testing (UAT) is the formal testing that is performed by the business users, who know the data better than anyone else. Their participation is critical for ensuring that the system being rolled into production has been thoroughly tested and, therefore, will not cause issues. The UAT is a formal process, which is implemented according to a well-defined plan that focuses only on the front end—not the ETL process.

After the UAT is concluded successfully, the UAT lead signs off to confirm that the reporting system is accurate and works as expected. During UAT, reports and dashboards are tested. If there is any error, an issue is logged. The development team then reviews the problem and applies the appropriate fix. The report is then retested. After all reports identified for UAT testing are passed, the UAT is declared successful and presented for sign-off by the UAT test lead and the business.

473 What type of testing is performed during UAT?

The testing scope typically includes validation of some or all reports, dashboards, scorecards, layout of individual reports, data within individual reports, totals and subtotals, drill-downs, hierarchies, filters, rollups and aggregates, as well as security by reports and roles. Also tested is data integrity after transfer, conversion, or updates. The objective is to ensure that data has been transferred between the systems completely and accurately.

474 Who participates in UAT?

There are usually five different types of resources who participate in UAT:

- UAT test lead
- Business analysts
- Business leads
- Testers
- IT representatives

475 What are the UAT roles and responsibilities?

The UAT test lead, who is responsible for UAT execution, coordinates between the business and IT to ensure that it is planned and executed successfully. The tasks performed by the test lead include working with IT to ensure the availability of infrastructure/systems, provide testers with the proper authorization and access, monitor issues that impact testing, monitor the resolution of bugs and fixes, lead coordination and status tracking meetings with the business leads, track overall progress, and provide status reports to management.

The business analysts perform many tasks, including creating test cases and scenarios as well as working with the business leads and testers to resolve application issues, data issues, and bugs. They also, as needed, coordinate with the data source system resources to resolve issues. The testers execute and test specific reports, dashboards, or scenarios assigned to them, log defects and issues, document deviations and/or bugs, and provide daily status to the business leads.

The business functional lead is responsible for identifying the reports to be tested, writing test cases and scenarios, selecting testers and assigning them to individual reports and/or test cases, planning the testing schedule, managing and coordinating resources, monitoring the testing progress, reviewing bugs and issues, assigning defects and bugs to specific groups and/or individuals, prioritizing defects, approving any workarounds, and providing daily status reports to the UAT test lead. The business lead provides the certification that the system is defect-free and meets the specifications and, finally, signs off to approve and certify that the UAT has been completed successfully.

476 What is the IT role in UAT?

The IT department has many responsibilities during the execution of UAT. It creates and maintains the QA environment, where the testing is conducted, that closely matches the production environment. It loads the data required for testing prior to the start of UAT. It is responsible for ensuring data integrity, managing security and authorizations, executing data refreshes as scheduled or when requested, monitoring defects and issues that are logged, troubleshooting technical issues (data or reports), monitoring the system to ensure optimal system performance, as well as moving tested software into production.

477 What should be avoided during testing?

Many reasons can cause testing to fail. The following are a few tips that can help avoid testing issues and failures:

- Actively involve the business users.
- Avoid using testers who have limited experience or who are not familiar with the functional process.
- Use real data—not sample data.
- Do not focus only on testing reports—data testing is very important.
- Validate data warehouse results/data with corresponding results/data in the source system.
- Allocate adequate time for testing, bug fixing, and regression testing.
- Specify the pass/fail criteria to be used—for individual items as well as the overall testing.
- Always obtain sign-offs after the testing is completed.

478 Who needs to be trained?

Depending on their current skills, as well as the infrastructure components that are to be installed or upgraded, project team members, including functional and IT staff, might need tailored training. Power users as well as end-users must also be provided with adequate and timely training. If the end-users are not well trained, the acceptance level of the system, and its utilization, will be less than desired.

479 What type of training needs to be delivered?

The needs of most casual users, who typically run canned reports, differ considerably from those of power users and business analysts who need to mine the data warehouse in innovative ways. Training should be tailored so that it meets the requirements of all users, whose skill levels vary significantly. The overall training can encompass the installation as well as the use of tools such as the ETL tool, front-end tool, database, monitoring and control software, metadata, data-modeling tool, and others.

End-users will perhaps need training in some or all of the following topics:

- Accessing the front-end tool (desktop and/or Web)
- Navigating using the front-end tool
- Creating and modifying queries
- Using basic analysis techniques
- Using advanced analysis techniques
- Browsing through the metadata
- Using specific types of data
- Using the data dictionary
- Creating alerts
- Navigating dashboards
- Analyzing scorecards

CHAPTER 46

DEPLOYMENT AND OPERATION

480 Should inadequate attention to deployment be of any concern?

The design and construction phases receive the maximum attention during a data warehouse implementation project. In some cases, however, the actual deployment does not get the attention it deserves even though it is an important and challenging task. When deployment problems arise, they can lead to the perception that the project is less than successful despite it running very smoothly during the UAT phase. In extreme cases, it can cause the data warehouse to be viewed very negatively by the users and, consequently, can create an acceptance issue.

481 What is involved in the final preparation before go-live?

After the UAT has been signed off, the final preparation for go-live begins. A number of prerequisite tasks, some minor, are required to be completed for this milestone. Some of them can be implemented prior to UAT, whereas others can be executed after the testing phase has been completed. There are several important tasks to be performed:

- Adding users to the system
- Assigning roles to all users
- Communicating login information
- Providing instructions for accessing the system

- Installing or upgrading infrastructure components, such as network, computers, mobile devices, etc.
- Getting user desktops ready
- Installing the front-end tool on individual desktops
- Creating and publishing queries and reports
- Delivering end-user training
- Establishing a support structure, including the tool for logging issues
- Establishing a change control process
- Switching off the legacy system, if the new system is a replacement
- Communicating relevant information about data loading, logging issues, etc.

482 What is involved in readiness assessment?

Readiness assessment is an important task that aims to determine whether the users as well as the system are ready for rollout into production. Typically, for this purpose, a project management meeting is conducted, in which a checklist is reviewed to confirm the completion of critical items. After the checklist has been reviewed, a risk evaluation is performed and a "go" or "no go" decision is made. If it is decided to move ahead, a number of communications, with different messages, are transmitted to everyone associated with the project.

483 What are the benefits of deploying in phases?

There are many benefits of deploying the data warehouse in phases:

- Risk is reduced.
- Experience is gained in dimensional modeling.
- Experience is gained in ETL on a smaller scale.
- Project cost is spread out.

- Users are brought online in a phased manner.
- Users gain experience in technologies and tools with which they are unfamiliar.
- Functionality can be rolled out in phases.
- Mistakes will be limited and easier to rectify.
- Learning opportunity is provided for those without experience.
- There are fewer resource constraints.
- Business users and priorities are more easily managed.

484 What are common rollout issues?

Some rollouts are very smooth, whereas others are plagued by a broad range of issues. Some of the common problems include login issues, inability to access data because of incorrect security profile, poor training, Help Desk inadequately staffed or trained, missing reports, slow performance, inability to drill down, unexpected results are returned, and other challenges.

485 What is involved in operating the data warehouse?

After the data warehouse becomes operational, the data management process, including extraction, transformation, staging, and load scheduling is automated, wherever possible. The loading is scheduled based on one of two common procedures: bulk download (which refreshes the entire database periodically) and change-based replication (which copies the differences in data residing on different servers).

Once a data warehouse is up and running, it will continue to require attention in different ways. A successful data warehouse will see the numbers of users rise considerably, which can affect its performance—if it has not been properly sized. Also, support and enhancement requests will roll in. Some other common tasks and issues that need to be dealt with while operating a data warehouse are as follows:

- Adding new sources
- Modifying existing sources feeding the data warehouse

- Loading new data on a regular basis, which can range from real time to weekly
- Managing batch-loading jobs; resolving loading errors
- Making changes in scheduling of data updates
- Updating data to reflect organizational changes, mergers, and acquisitions
- Performing mapping and loading modifications due to source system changes
- Making changes in data ownership
- Ensuring uptime and reliability
- Resolving performance issues
- Managing the front-end tools
- Managing the back-end components
- Requesting modifying reports
- Applying fixes for report, dashboard, and distribution issues
- Reconciling reports because of changes in existing reports
- Creating and/or updating dashboards and scorecards
- Managing user accounts—adding new users, etc.
- Handling security issues
- Changing security profiles due to role changes
- Tuning for optimal performance
- Monitoring processing times for queries
- Handling changes in management and process for approvals
- Migrating reports and other objects from the QA system into production
- Effecting disaster recovery
- Creating backups and archiving

- Upgrading software
- Other support issues

486 Do data warehouse projects ever end?

The belief that issues will stop generating once a data warehouse project is up and running is misguided. After a data warehouse goes live, users continue to ask for more data marts, enhancements, custom or additional reports, additional data (more fields and/or longer periods), and so forth. Therefore, the data warehouse environment will always be dynamic.

487 How are enhancements handled?

As users become more familiar with the data warehouse, and start to appreciate its powerful and flexible features and functions, they demand enhancements and more data. The more successful the data warehouse, the faster new requirements will come in. The best way to handle such requests is to steer them through a change control process. If the system has been well designed and is flexible and scalable, there should be few issues in handling even a large number of requests.

488 What type of support is to be provided?

Support is usually provided using a tiered approach. The first level comprises the power users within the user's group. If they are unable to resolve the issue, it is escalated to the super user level. If the issue is not resolved at that level, then it is escalated, via the Help Desk, to IT, which has the technical expertise to resolve data warehouse issues, especially if they pertain to data. If IT is unable to resolve a really complex issue, then an attempt is made to resolve it jointly (by business and IT).

CHAPTER 47

TRENDS

489 Scalability

The amount of data collected by enterprises has grown exponentially in the past couple of decades. An important part of this data has been moved into data warehouses and decision-support systems so that it can be analyzed. In contrast to transaction data, which used to be archived after a couple of years, this data continues to be retained in systems where it can be accessed and analyzed easily.

Together with the explosion in data volumes, the number of users has also increased exponentially and is expected to continue growing for the foreseeable future. This means that the infrastructure, hardware, and software required to support the growing data volumes and users will also need to keep pace. Hence, designing for scalability will continue to remain an important planning and design issue.

490 Number and variety of data sources will continue to expand

Initially data warehouses were populated from legacy mainframes or ERP systems. Now they are being fed from a variety of sources such as CRM systems, Internet, clickstream data, data marts and data warehouses, smartphones, demographic data, external financial data, third-part data, and others. It is expected that the number of data sources, as well as their variety, will continue to grow rapidly.

491 Hardware, database, and architecture enhancements

The accumulation of huge volumes of data has placed strains on the hardware required to support it. For processing the huge volumes of stored data, various technologies have been introduced or widely applied. These include faster and more powerful hardware, data warehouse appliances, in-memory solutions with data caches, columnar databases, open-source databases, in-memory and column-store DBMSs, data hubs, performance optimization, as well as massively parallel processors (MPPs), which can significantly improve data loading, index creation, and query processing. This trend of enhancements in hardware, databases, and architecture will continue.

492 Integration

Integration can be manifested in different ways. Database vendors have enhanced their product features to integrate multidimensional tools and OLAP functionality into their flagship products. Analytical tools are being integrated with databases to enhance performance. Integration is also manifested in the following ways:

- Enterprise data integration
  - Although a data warehouse's basic objective is enterprise integration, there is room for improvement so that it is pervasive and seamless, leveraging newer tools such as MDM. A technique, fusion, still in its infancy, has the potential to provide many benefits by providing the ability to merge data from different sources.
- Integration with OLTP systems
  - There is tighter and seamless integration between the data warehouses and their source systems, like ERP and CRM. This will make ETL procedures simpler, faster, and more reliable.
- Integration across platforms
  - With the architecture forced to support many components from different vendors, there will be continued effort to integrate platforms, components, and tools. The integration push, across systems and vendors, will cross the complete landscape and be supported through collaborative efforts.

- Integration across applications
  - There is support of comprehensive analysis, such as for customers, through integration and accuracy across applications, data sources, organization units, and various dimensions (such as regions and channels).
- Integration with social media
  - This involves the ability to use information and interaction occurring in various social media environments, such as Facebook.
- Integration with social computing media
  - This includes leveraging of unstructured data, such as texts and Twitter, to provide analytics.

493 Real-time integration and decision making

Because of the pressure to improve decision making, there is, and will continue to be, a move toward an environment that supports real-time integration (between data warehouses and operational systems), analysis, and decision making. This feature is also known as "Active Data Warehouse." It can be achieved only through very tight integration between the data warehouse and its source operational systems, which will enable access to historical as well as current detailed data in real-time or near-real-time mode. The integration will enable the support of both operational and strategic needs. It will also enable automated decisions and event-driven actions, which will be based on data that is actionable.

494 SaaS and cloud computing

Business intelligence will become available as a service. Business intelligence access and delivery through SaaS and cloud, or Internet-based, computing will increase and become quite common. The trend toward thin clients and remote access will continue. The benefit of Web access to the data warehouse is that it will provide remote analysis capabilities and, also, enable data in the target database to be refreshed through the Web. There are other benefits of SaaS and cloud computing, as well:

- Easy access
- Easy deployment
- Sharing of resources
- Accessibility
- Standardization
- Cost
- Low installation and maintenance for enabling access
- Scalability
- Platform independence
- Automated provisioning

It is expected that bundled products such as Web servers, access tools, and databases will become widely available and upgrades will be simplified.

Mobile BI, or access to business intelligence through mobile devices such as smartphones, will increase significantly. Technologies such as Service Oriented Architecture (SOA) Interfaces, also known as Interface-Oriented Architecture, will be used extensively as they can integrate multiple platforms and disparate applications in a Web-based environment.

495 Advanced analytics

Because of the demand to get the maximum benefit out of data warehouses, major improvements in analytical tools are expected. A variety of tools will become available because no single tool can be expected to meet all the needs of an organization. These tools are expected to be closely integrated with the database. Other trends in this area focus on specific tools and techniques:

- OLAP and data mining
- Web-enabling front-end tools

- Analysis across data marts, different platforms, and heterogeneous data sources
- Handling more complex queries
- Real-time event triggers and repository monitoring
- Predictive analytics
- In-memory analysis
- Leveraging parallelism

496 Unstructured data analysis and merge capabilities

The focus until now has been on the analysis of structured data, which has historically been loaded into data warehouses. There is, however, a move toward utilizing unstructured data such as text, which companies now want to analyze and act on. With the ability to bridge the gulf between structured and unstructured data, users will have additional advanced analytical and decision-making capabilities.

497 Governance

There will be a push for more data and business intelligence governance. The key focus is on data quality, which must be maintained at a high level to support reliable and effective analytics. Governance initiatives will ensure that the goals for data quality are set and achieved. They will also enable the availability of the appropriate tools, such as MDM, for meeting those goals.

498 Improvements in agent technology

Agents are tools to automate decision making and initiate actions, depending on certain triggers and analysis. For example, if the sales fall below a certain threshold on any day, the sales manager will receive an alert, which can be transmitted through various methods, highlighting the abnormal condition. At this time, agent technology is being used in a limited way. However, it has the potential to be refined, with built-in intelligence, and used in a more effective and timely fashion, which will cause its application and usage to increase.

499 Visualization

Visualization is the graphical or visual presentation of data, which is usually presented in dashboards and scorecards. Its objective is to provide users with information in a business context that can be displayed in various forms such as data, KPIs, processes, diagrams, charts, graphs, dials, maps, and so forth. The entities are usually interactive and, using different techniques, they can be drilled into or summarized, presented in multiple views, can display trends or show how data changed over time. The use of this technology is growing fast and will continue to do so in the future.

500 More intelligence and technologies will be built in

There has been a move away from the enterprise data warehouse being a stand-alone repository, against which analysis used to be performed. If the present trend continues, the EDW will see more technologies and intelligence built into it, so that it becomes more versatile. For example, it will be able to find relevant data, as and when needed, from a single or multiple sources (static or streaming); analyze it; and then push it into the applications where the results of the analysis can be incorporated and utilized.

Complex event processing, where data streams containing numerous variables can be analyzed and used for decision making, will influence business intelligence by enabling operational data to be analyzed and acted on for automated decision support. For example, Sybase, which was acquired by SAP, uses this technology to dynamically monitor real-time data and, in response to anticipated or changed conditions, trigger appropriate alerts. Semantic technologies, currently being used in many environments (such as hospitals), are expected to be applied more widely. The technologies can enable reconciliation, such as for business definitions, across various data sources and content.

INDEX